Bahá'í Families

Perspectives, Principles, Practice

by

PATRICIA WILCOX

GR

GEORGE RONALD

OXFORD

George Ronald, Publisher
46 High Street, Kidlington, Oxford OX5 2DN

British Library Cataloguing in Publication Data
Wilcox, Patricia
    Bahá'í families: Perspectives, principles,
    practice.
    I. Title
    306.8508

        ISBN 0–85398–331–3

Contents

He that bringeth up his son or the son of another,
it is as though he hath brought up a son of Mine;
upon him rest My Glory, My loving-kindness, my Mercy,
that have compassed the world.

BAHÁ'U'LLÁH

Foreword

Although the New Zealand Bahá'í community in which I live is very diverse in character, two factors are common to all members: we have all been children and we have all lived in families. Many of us are also parents. Consequently, our concerns about Bahá'í family life and the education of children are frequent topics of our consultations, both formal and informal.

I have written this book to give expression to the many valuable and constructive insights which I have gathered from my fellow Bahá'ís and from my own study of the Bahá'í Writings, and which have been verified in my experience as a teacher, family counsellor, child and parent.

Every family is a unique creation, reflecting the great diversity of humankind. In selecting examples to illustrate various points, it was difficult to reflect adequately the range of cultural, economic and national differences. Consequently I have tended to use examples which reflect my own Bahá'í community. I trust that the reader will appreciate the limitations of these and substitute in their place more personally appropriate examples.

In the absence of one inclusive term which embraces male and female, in this book the male pronoun is often used in its generic sense to include both, thus following

the precedent set in English-language works of the Central
Figures of the Faith.

Patricia Wilcox
Hamilton, New Zealand 1991

Acknowledgements

I am forever indebted to my parents who gave me life and taught me that the fundamental purpose of the family is to know and love God. I am extremely grateful for the support and encouragement of my husband, Alan, and my children – Joanne, Jamie, Megan, Daniel and John – through whom I learned a great deal about Bahá'í family life. I also thank my extended family, especially Suzanne Worters, my teacher, and Nancy Dobrochowski, whose editorial skills were so valuable.

Finally, I wish to thank George Ronald, Publisher for their confidence, and especially Wendi Momen whose guidance and support sustained me in my solitary hours at the keyboard.

I

Introductory Perspectives

The Bahá'í Family: A Fortress for Well-Being

When two people marry they set about creating a family unit. Each one has an idea of what a family should be. Where do these ideas generally come from? Until we become Bahá'ís our own families often provide most of the model; we keep the things we liked most about our families and vow never to be like our parents in the things we didn't like. We also copy bits from movies, television, magazines, books and the examples of other people. We then put them all together and try to muddle through as best we can in the absence of any specialized instruction in 'how to parent'.

In this sense we are pioneers of the Bahá'í family, exploring what is still pretty much an unknown quantity and breaking new ground. But we Bahá'ís have one immeasurable advantage over the generality of human-kind: our understanding of the rights, responsibilities and principles of parenthood is no random patchwork of vague impressions and aspirations but is based upon the priceless storehouse of divine guidance within the Bahá'í Writings.

The example set by parents provides the most important foundation in preparing children for their future parenthood. Whatever a child sees being practised in the home will become necessary and natural to him or her. For first generation Bahá'í parents this is at once an unparalleled task and a unique bounty. On the one hand, we must begin from scratch, without the benefit of immediate role models, to realize in our families the principles of the Faith. On the other hand, if we set a befittingly high standard, our children will effortlessly accept these ordinances as part of everyday life. For this reason the greatest, most important, responsibility of a Bahá'í parent is to 'live the life'. We are told that the only way to ensure success in teaching the Cause is to live the life. Parenting is teaching the Cause: bringing forth one who will make mention of God. Parenting is living the life: letting deeds, not words, be our adorning. Whatever words we speak concerning the glorious principles of our Faith, it will be our day by day standards of hospitality, consultation, prayer, avoidance of backbiting, giving to the fund and so forth that will create lasting impressions in the minds of our children. Therefore, in whatever way we seek to educate and develop our children, let us first call ourselves to account and adjust our lives accordingly.

The Bedrock upon which to Build the Fortress[1]

In many places the Bahá'í Writings liken the institutions of the Faith to buildings. Different aspects are described as fortresses, edifaces, pillars, domes, houses and foundations. The Spiritual Assemblies are Houses of Justice. The family is a fortress.

Every builder knows that the first condition needed in the erection of a building is a strong foundation. Christ used the analogy of a building to illustrate how His teachings would provide a strong and secure foundation in the lives of those who lived according to them:

What then of the man who hears these words of mine and acts upon them? He is like a man who had the sense to build his house on rock. The rain came down, the floods rose, the wind blew, and beat upon that house; but it did not fall, because its foundations were on rock. But what of the man who hears these words of mine and does not act upon them? He is like a man who was foolish enough to build his house on sand. The rain came down, the floods rose, the wind blew, and beat upon that house; down it fell with a great crash.[2]

Likening the family to a fortress suggests that the family will be subjected to strong outside pressures and forces. The Guardian of the Bahá'í Faith, Shoghi Effendi, warns us of these pressures and advises us on how we can combat them.

The Bahá'ís must, through rigid adherence to the Bahá'í laws and teachings, combat these corrosive forces which are so rapidly destroying home life and the beauty of family relationships, and tearing down the moral structure of society.[3]

The Bahá'í laws and teachings constitute a bedrock upon which secure and strong families can be established. Bedrock is defined in *Webster's New Collegiate Dictionary* as 'the solid rock underlying superficial formations', 'a solid foundation', and 'the lowest level'. The Guardian identifies several items which constitute the bedrock upon which the institutions of the Administrative Order should be built:

The bedrock on which this Administrative Order is founded is God's immutable Purpose for mankind in this day.[4]

. . . the permanent welfare of the Faith demands the steady development of local Bahá'í community life [which] is the bedrock of Bahá'í national growth and development.[5]

. . . the bedrock of the Bahá'í administrative order is the
principle of unity in diversity . . . [6]

Consultation, frank and unfettered, is the bedrock of this
unique order.[7]

. . . those basic and distinguishing principles of [the] Faith
. . . together with the laws and ordinances . . . constitute
the bed-rock of God's latest Revelation to mankind.[8]

God's Immutable Purpose for Mankind

The purpose of the family can be understood only in the
light of God's purpose for mankind as a whole. Each
family member is one of the countless links in the mighty
chain that girdles the globe, a brick in the administrative
structure, an instrument to be used by Bahá'u'lláh in the
execution of the Divine Plan.

It is the task of marriage partners to foster harmony and
unity and to bring forth children so that successive
generations will fulfil God's purpose for humankind. The
family both educates and serves. It assists and promotes
the development of each member in the personal process
of learning to know and love God. The short Obligatory
Prayer describes this as the purpose of our creation.

The following chapter will establish the purpose of the
family within the larger context of the World Order.
Successive sections will consider ways in which the family
can manifest this purpose through the development of
greater levels of knowledge of God's Will for the family,
consultation, planning and action.

Bahá'í Community Life

A feature of Bahá'í life is the strong interdependence
which exists between the family and the community.
They are bound by strong spiritual ties of fellowship,

cooperation and unity of purpose. The social life of a united Bahá'í community exerts a powerful attraction. Associating with fellow believers strengthens the Bahá'í identity of the individual, enkindles spirits and promotes the benefits of diversity through shared strengths, talents and resources.

The community is a microcosm of the world. The skills and qualities which are required to foster international cooperation and fellowship – equality, freedom from prejudice, justice, consultation and so forth – are learned in the family, applied in the community and ultimately benefit the world. Following sections will consider the relationship of the family to the community in greater depth.

Unity in Diversity

The family is a community with extremely diverse members. Within the family is diversity of sex, age, background, talent, capacity and, in some cases, race, colour and culture. According to the Bahá'í Writings there is also diversity of rights and responsibilities: the father, mother and children each have their own particular ones. A chapter of this book will focus on the principle of unity in diversity within the family and suggest ways in which this may be achieved. In addition, a chapter on education will examine the particular requirements and responsibilities of the mother and father as educators.

Consultation

The process through which the Universal House of Justice is informed of, and responds to, the needs of a world community is the same process followed by the smallest community, the family. In fact, it is within the family that the first, most important, consultation skills are learned. So vital is the role of consultation that it has been described as essential to welfare and well-being, to be observed by all, the cause of awareness and awakening, the bestower of understanding and the lamp of guidance.

In acknowledgement of the essential and fundamental nature of consultation, a chapter of this book is devoted to the purpose and application of consultation within the family, and reference is made to it in many other sections.

Basic Principles, Laws and Ordinances

Most of the manifold principles, laws and ordinances of the Faith have either a direct or an indirect bearing upon the family. In this book some major principles – consultation and unity in diversity – are the subjects of complete chapters. Others are referred to as they relate to specific areas of content. A consistent emphasis is upon translating knowledge of these principles, laws and ordinances into action. For this reason consideration is given to the setting of goals and, whenever possible, to practical suggestions for implementing ideas.

One Bedrock, Diverse Buildings

All the institutions of the Faith are built upon the same bedrock. All function according to one set of principles. All are carrying forward God's immutable purpose for humanity. However, the institutions differ in their expressions of this purpose, according to the needs of those they serve. The function of the Universal House of Justice differs from the function of the family. Similarly, each family serves a different group of individuals with different needs, capacities and environments. The factors which are unique to the individual family include the talents, skills and occupations of individual members, level of wealth, culture, area of Bahá'í service and needs of the surrounding community.

For this reason, it is impossible to describe the definitive Bahá'í family. Each is unique, each is growing and changing. The common factor is the bedrock upon which the foundations of each family are firmly anchored.

2

The Place of the Family in the World Order

The foundation of the Bahá'í family is marriage. The family is the smallest unit of a world community; therefore, marriage is of great importance to world civilization. Stable, united, spiritualized marriages will produce those qualities within their families and, ultimately, within the world.

It is difficult for Bahá'ís to appreciate fully the reality of Bahá'í marriage when we are part of a society with such different views. In many cultures, weddings are primarily romantic occasions of flowers, music, poetry, expensive gifts and pretty dresses, or they are opportunities for excessive eating and drinking, ribald jokes and wild partying. The marriage is viewed as a convenient association between two people, which may or may not work out, and which offers divorce as a convenient and relatively easy escape.

In contrast, Bahá'í marriage is described in various parts of the Writings as a law, a command, a covenant. The very essence of Bahá'í marriage is the making of a strong covenant between the partners in the sight of God. The marriage ceremony itself is deceptively simple, requiring only that each party recite the verse

We will all, verily, abide by the Will of God.

Although brief, the Bahá'í marriage vow – to abide by the Will of God – is vast in its intention, sweeping in its range, and weighty in its responsibility. Several significant concepts are implicit in this vow:

- The promise to abide by the Will of God establishes the family firmly upon the bedrock of God's immutable purpose for humanity: the marriage partners express their intention to fulfil their part in God's Will and purpose.

- A corollary of this is that the partners need, both as a preparation for marriage and then as an on-going process throughout their lives together, to become well-informed about the nature of God's purpose for humankind.

- The intention to abide by the Will of God links the marriage inseparably to the other institutions of the Faith which are charged with the same responsibility: to carry out the Will of God on earth, to fulfil their part in God's purpose for humankind.

The Significance of the Marriage Vow to the World Order

The World Order of Bahá'u'lláh describes the way in which individuals unite in a series of systematic and mutually supportive institutions which reach out to embrace all corners of the world with one purpose: to carry out the Will of God on earth. They are like the building blocks of a vast and mighty fortress for the well-being and salvation of the whole planet.

Each level of the World Order is founded on a covenant: an acknowledgement of one's spiritual obligations and a pledge to fulfil those obligations in the sight of God:

- The individual Bahá'í makes a declaration of belief and obedience.

- The institution of the family is founded on the marriage vow, a declaration that the partners will abide by the Will of God. In making this covenant, the partners, by implication, further pledge to raise their children to be obedient to their parents, who are themselves pledged to abide by the Will of God. It follows that the children will be brought up in obedience to the commands of God. That is, children will be brought up to be obedient both to their parents and to God and will abide by God's Will.

- The institution of the Local Spiritual Assembly is founded on a Declaration of Trust. Article I of the By-Laws of a Local Spiritual Assembly states: 'The Trustees . . . acknowledge for themselves and on behalf of their successors the sacred meaning and universal purpose of the Bahá'í Faith, the teachings and principles of which fulfil the divine promise of all former revealed religions.'[1]

- The institution of the National Spiritual Assembly is founded on the explicit teachings of Bahá'u'lláh as expressed in the Declaration of Trust. In that document, the Assembly pledges to exercise, administer and carry on the powers, responsibilities, rights, privileges and obligations given it by Bahá'u'lláh, 'Abdu'l-Bahá, Shoghi Effendi and the Universal House of Justice.

- The institution of the Universal House of Justice is founded on a Declaration of Trust pledging 'to ensure the continuity of that divinely-appointed authority which flows from the Source of the Faith, to safeguard the unity of its followers, and to maintain the integrity and flexibility of its teachings'.[2]

Common Functions of the Institutions of the Faith

In addition to being founded upon binding covenants, there are many similarities in the functions of the institutions. A letter written on behalf of the Guardian states:

> . . . he feels that you should turn to your local Assembly . . . and seek their aid and advice. These bodies have the sacred obligation to help, advise, protect and guide the believers . . . You should go to them as a child would to its parents . . . [3]

Therefore, the marriage partners are parents to the children. The Local Spiritual Assembly functions as a parent to the local community, the National Spiritual Assembly as a parent to the nation, and the Universal House of Justice as a parent to humanity, an embodiment of God the Father on earth. All of these great institutions act as loving parents. All have the sacred obligation to help, advise, protect and guide those they serve. They share the purpose of maintaining order, unity and obedience to the Cause of God. They promote the education and enlightenment of those they serve and they all function through the process of consultation. They command obedience from all levels below them and obey all levels above: the children within the family unit must obey the parents, the family must obey the Local Assembly and so forth.

As humanity moves out of an old age and into a new one, an age the like of which history has never known and which even now can only dimly be discerned, traditional ways of life are found to be inadequate to meet the needs of the time. The followers of Bahá'u'lláh are embarking upon a process of transformation – of themselves, their families and their communities.

Within the Writings of Bahá'u'lláh is the blueprint for

the society of the future. We are called upon to establish institutions which will form the framework of future civilization.

Each institution is a new creation, unlike anything humankind has ever known. It is as if we were building a unique and astonishing structure; we are the builders, Bahá'u'lláh is the artchitect and our blueprint is the Writings. The successive plans launched by the Guardian and the Universal House of Justice chart the gradual development of these institutions and set forth the various tasks for immediate attention. One of these tasks is 'the nurturing of a deeper understanding of Bahá'í family life'.[4]

The Bahá'í concept of family is unique. 'Abdu'l-Bahá demonstrates how this understanding applies to many different levels of humanity:

> Compare the nations of the world to the members of a family. A family is a nation in miniature. Simply enlarge the circle of the household, and you have the nation. Enlarge the circle of nations, and you have all humanity. The conditions surrounding the family surround the nation. The happenings in the family are the happenings in the life of the nation. Would it add to the progress and advancement of a family if dissensions should arise among its members, all fighting, pillaging each other, jealous and revengeful of injury, seeking selfish advantage? Nay, this would be the cause of the effacement of progress and advancement. So it is in the great family of nations, for nations are but an aggregate of families.[5]

The popular idea portrayed in the media of the family as a self-subsistent, materialistic consumer unit bears no resemblance at all to the Bahá'í family which is a spiritual creation and part of a system of divinely-ordained institutions. This, then, is the context in which the individual Bahá'í family can be viewed: as one brick in the mighty edifice of mankind, as one leaf upon the tree of humanity.

When each family supports whole-heartedly, continuously and generously the plans and ideals of the National Spiritual Assemblies, the world community is correspondingly strengthened. The members of the Bahá'í family see all humanity as brothers and sisters:

> The spiritual brotherhood which is enkindled and established through the breaths of the Holy Spirit unites nations and removes the cause of warfare and strife. It transforms mankind into one great family and establishes the foundations of the oneness of humanity. It promulgates the spirit of international agreement and ensures universal peace. Therefore, we must investigate the foundation of this heavenly fraternity. We must forsake all imitations and promote the reality of the divine teachings. In accordance with these principles and actions and by the assistance of the Holy Spirit, both material and spiritual happiness shall become realized.[6]

The Role of the Individual

Although we know that the fundamental teaching of the Faith is unity, it is only as we develop spiritually as individuals that we recognize more and more the pervasive oneness of the world of creation. The following statement from Shoghi Effendi describes the importance of the part – the individual – to the whole:

> He it is who constitutes the warp and woof on which the quality and pattern of the whole fabric must depend. He it is who acts as one of the countless links in the mighty chain that now girdles the globe. He it is who serves as one of the multitude of bricks which support the structure and ensure the stability of the administrative edifice now being raised in every part of the world. Without his support, at once whole-hearted, continuous and generous, every measure adopted, and every plan formulated, by the body which acts as the national representative of the community to

which he belongs is foredoomed to failure. The World Centre of the Faith itself is paralyzed if such a support on the part of the rank and file of the community is denied it. The Author of the Divine Plan Himself is impeded in His purpose if the proper instruments for the execution of His design are lacking. The sustaining strength of Bahá'u'lláh Himself, the Founder of the Faith, will be withheld from every and each individual who fails in the long run to arise and play his part.[7]

Bahá'ís recognize that individual freedom, happiness and salvation can be found only in the harmony of the planet as a whole, for such are the inextricable links of interdependency that bind us together. The thoughts and actions of the individual family should not be directed merely at the selfish advancement of the individuals which comprise it but rather towards the betterment of human-kind as a whole.

The Special Unity between Husband and Wife

One of the greatest forms of unity is that between husband and wife. In fact, so great is the unity of true Bahá'í marriage that 'Abdu'l-Bahá says that the partners become even as one soul. His wish is that Bahá'í marriages will come to:

- embody 'the signs of harmony and unity until the end of time'[8]

- become 'the means of attracting perpetual grace'[9]

- enable the partners to foster harmony, fellowship and unity and to attain everlasting life.[10]

The power to achieve such harmony and unity that it can make two people even as one soul is the power of the

Covenant. The power that binds each of us into one family unit, the power that will eventually bind nations together into the family of humankind is the power of the Covenant.

The marriage covenant or vow is made by two people who express, not the intention of an individual – 'I will abide by the Will of God' – but the intention on behalf of both – '*We* will abide by the Will of God'. This implies a sense of joint responsibility for each other, a commitment to assist and enable one another to abide by God's Will.

> The true marriage of Bahá'í is this, that husband and wife should be united both physically and spiritually, that they may ever improve the spiritual life of each other, and may enjoy everlasting unity throughout all the worlds of God. This is Bahá'í marriage.[11]

When we as individual Bahá'ís declare our belief in Bahá'u'lláh, we make a binding personal commitment to be obedient to the Will of God as expressed through His Manifestation. In this way the spiritual growth and development of the individual is assured. When we as individual Bahá'ís marry, we then assume a certain responsibility for the spiritual growth and progress of our partners, in addition to being responsible for our own progress. This is true unity, that as one marriage partner we should care as much for the material and spiritual needs of our partner as for our own.

In describing the purpose of marriage, Bahá'u'lláh said:

> And when He desired to manifest grace and beneficence to men, and to set the world in order, He revealed observances and created laws; among them He established the law of marriage, made it as a fortress for well-being and salvation, and enjoined it upon us in that which was sent down out of the heaven of sanctity in His Most Holy Book. He saith, great is His glory: 'Marry, O people, that from you may

appear he who will remember Me amongst My servants; this is one of My commandments unto you; obey it as an assistance to yourselves.'[12]

Therefore, we obey the law of marriage because of the assistance it offers to us. There are three major benefits which we receive:

1. Marriage is as a *fortress for well-being and salvation*. It promises protection, shelter and the provision of what is necessary for human well-being and happiness, while enabling the partners to play a full part in the outside world.

2. The *children* born of the marriage are reared in a safe, nurturing environment and will be the means of promoting the Cause of God through future ages.

3. The establishment of strong harmonious marriages provides a firm foundation on which to build a *world order* by:

   • creating strong bonds of fellowship and obedience with the other institutions of the Faith, of which the family is the foundation stone.

   • giving the members a supportive environment in which to learn and practise the skills and virtues necessary to a peaceful, ordered world: consultation, forbearance, forgiveness, cooperation, etc. In the family we first begin to practise the fundamental teaching of all religions: to love one another as we love ourselves.

The Unity of the Family takes Priority

. . . the House of Justice points out that the unity of your family should take priority over any other consideration

. . . For example, service to the Cause should not produce neglect of the family. It is important for you to arrange your time so that your family life is harmonious and your household receives the attention it requires.[13]

This does not preclude members of a family voluntarily choosing to sacrifice their own interests for something they consider more important; but sacrifice must be a gift, it cannot be expected or taken. It is misguided for any family member to create disunity in the home under the mistaken idea that his or her aim is some greater social good to which the family must be subordinate. A weak family is a source of strength to no one. It is more likely that it will eventually become in need of the support of others. The equation here is that a strong marriage equals a strong family, strong families equal strong communities, and strong communities strengthen all humanity. Although it may be extremely frustrating, for example, to forego an exciting and promising activity because there is some matter in the family requiring attention, we must bear in mind the organic nature of the Cause: a plant can never produce more foliage or fruit than its root system is capable of supporting. If it tries to do so, the entire plant will risk being completely uprooted and destroyed. 'Abdu'l-Bahá explains:

Note ye how easily, where unity existeth in a given family, the affairs of that family are conducted; what progress the members of that family make, how they prosper in the world. Their concerns are in order, they enjoy comfort and tranquillity, they are secure, their position is assured, they come to be envied by all. Such a family but addeth to its stature and its lasting honour, as day succeedeth day.[14]

The Relationship of the Family to the Community

The larger community is really a composite of family

units, a sort of 'compound' family. Whilst the community functions according to precisely the same set of principles and values as the family unit, it expresses them in a broader sense. For example, the 'parent body' of the community, the Local Spiritual Assembly, will concern itself with such matters as the provision of child education programmes, community deepenings, firesides and travel teaching projects which enlist the support and provide for the betterment of the individual family unit.

However whilst in one sense it is true to say that the Bahá'ís of a community are one big family, this is a spiritual description; it describes an attitude of mutual love, care and support. It does not, for example, mean that we can freely avail ourselves of one another's property or time or hospitality, for these considerations must always be dependent on the good pleasure of the people involved. In one sense, we are encouraged to be self-sufficient, so that rather than requiring support from others we are dependent on naught save God. In another sense, the Bahá'í family is the antithesis of self-sufficiency because its members recognize that their mutual happiness lies in working together with their fellows as parts of a body, as leaves of one tree, assisting one another to know and love God.

The Family: A Unit of Service to Humanity

A truly Bahá'í home is a true fortress upon which the Cause can rely while planning its campaigns. If . . . and . . . love each other and would like to marry, Shoghi Effendi does not wish them to think that by doing so they are depriving themselves of the privilege of service: in fact such a union will enhance their ability to serve. There is nothing more beautiful than to have young Bahá'ís marry and found truly Bahá'í homes, the type Bahá'u'lláh wishes them to be. Please give them both the Guardian's loving greetings.[15]

The family that is firmly grounded in the principles of the Faith – founded upon a strong marriage, unified amongst its members, deepened in the knowledge of God and His creation and advancing both materially and spiritually – will of its own volition seek expression of itself through service to society, teaching and advancing the principles of the Cause and thereby contributing to the welfare of all humanity. Unless this vital state is achieved, all other achievements lose significance, for the Bahá'í family exists only within the context of humanity as a whole; it is not an end in itself. Our station is that of a servant and our family life should equip us to fulfil this station even from childhood.

The Extended Family

The Bahá'í family does not refer only to a group of people with close blood ties. Rather, the reverse is true. Our ideal should be to see everyone as brother or sister, to love without distinction. If we love only our 'blood relatives', we will fail to love those who are not. 'Abdu'l-Bahá warns us that the fraternity of family, race or religion is usually productive of disagreement, enmity and hatred. What a radical departure from traditional concepts is the Bahá'í family, for we have been reared in a society that encourages us to place our blood brothers and sisters ahead of others; now we must begin to love without distinction. Bahá'u'lláh promises:

> He that bringeth up his son or the son of another, it is though he hath brought up a son of Mine; upon him rest My Glory, My Loving-Kindness, My Mercy, that have compassed the world.[16]

The Bahá'í Writings acknowledge both physical and spiritual parents and state that, whilst both are worthy of respect, the spiritual parent (i.e. the one who nurtures the spiritual life of the child) is the greater:

> The spiritual father is greater than the physical one, for the latter bestoweth but this world's life, whereas the former endoweth his child with life everlasting. This is why, in the Law of God, teachers are listed among the heirs.[17]

How fortunate are those of us who have had both types of nurturing from the same person! This concept of spiritual parenting has a broad effect: parent and child relationships are no longer dependent on blood ties. In the Bahá'í concept of family, step-parents, adoptive parents, foster parents and, in fact, any committed adults can, upon taking responsibility for the spiritual development of a child, know that they are, in the true sense, real parents. An extension of this reality is that through the act of teaching the Faith in our day-to-day lives, we are fulfilling an aspect of parenthood – a state embodied in the names bestowed upon those sterling antipodean teachers, Mother and Father Dunn. As the spirit of faith is awakened in the new believer, his or her spiritual parents (who may be individuals or even a whole community) must nurture that infant faith, and are responsible to God for the care of the 'spiritual child'.

Therefore, with the call continually to teach the Faith, each of us is in reality being called to search for souls in whom God has infused the spirit of the life of the Kingdom, to whom we must become spiritual parents. This parenting is the true parenting and has no end.

> Now you in reality have acquired all these spiritual children free and gratis, and that is better than having physical children; for such children are not grateful to their fathers, since they feel the father serveth them because he must – and therefore no matter what he doeth for them, they pay it no mind. Spiritual children, however, are always appreciative

of their father's loving-kindness. This verily is out of the grace of thy Lord, the Beneficent.[18]

The Holy Family

The Bahá'í family is unique and has no equivalent in all history. It is above and beyond blood ties and physical relationship, and describes both the single family unit and humanity as a whole. As members of this family, and the only members to have the blueprint for its ideal development, it is our responsibility to investigate its reality, become informed of the principles governing its development and then, by transforming these principles into reality in our day-to-day lives, to thereby ensure both our own material and spiritual happiness and that of all humankind. In the following chapters these principles will be examined and applied to the needs of the single family unit.

Bahá'ís treasure the stories of the early days of the Faith and, in particular, those stories which illustrate the lives of the Central Figures. Accounts which describe the family life of these Figures are few, so the following memories of Bahíyyih Khánum, the daughter of Bahá'u'lláh, are especially rare and precious. This account, and the two that follow, give us a glimpse of the unique character and qualities which we Bahá'ís are striving to embody within our families.

> My father was Mírzá Ḥusayn-'Alí of Núr, who married my beautiful mother, Ásíyih Khánum, when she was very young. She was the only daughter of a Persian Vizier, of high degree, Mírzá Ismá'íl. He, as well as Mírzá 'Abbás Buzurg, my paternal grandfather, possessed great wealth.
>
> When the brother of my mother married my father's sister, the double alliance of the two noble families roused much interest throughout the land. 'It is adding wealth to wealth', the people said. Ásíyih Khánum's wedding

treasures were extensive, in accordance with the usual custom in families of their standing; forty mules were loaded with her possessions when she came to her husband's home.

For six months before the marriage a jeweller worked at her home, preparing jewellery – even the buttons of her garments were of gold, set with precious stones. (These buttons were destined to be exchanged for bread, on the terrible exile journey from Ṭihrán to Baghdád.)

I wish you could have seen her as I first remember her, tall, slender, graceful, eyes of dark blue – a pearl, a flower amongst women.

I have been told that even when very young, her wisdom and intelligence were remarkable. I always think of her in those earliest days of my memory as queenly in her dignity and loveliness, full of consideration for everybody, gentle, of a marvellous unselfishness, no action of hers ever failed to show the loving-kindness of her pure heart; her very presence seemed to make an atmosphere of love and happiness wherever she came, enfolding all comers in the fragrance of gentle courtesy.

Even in the early days of their married life, they, my father and mother, took part as little as possible in State functions, social ceremonies, and the luxurious habits of ordinary highly-placed and wealthy families in the land of Persia; she, and her noble-hearted husband, counted these worldly pleasures meaningless, and preferred rather to occupy themselves in caring for the poor, and for all who were unhappy, or in trouble.

From our doors nobody was ever turned away; the hospitable board was spread for all comers.

Constantly the poor women came to my mother, to whom they poured out their various stories of woe, to be comforted and consoled by her loving helpfulness.

Whilst the people called my father 'The Father of the Poor', they spoke of my mother as 'The Mother of Consolation', though, naturally, only the women and little children ever looked upon her face unveiled.

So our peaceful days flowed on.

We used to go to our house in the country sometimes; my brother 'Abbás and I loved to play in the beautiful gardens, where grew many kinds of wonderful fruits and flowers and flowering trees; but this part of my early life is a very dim memory.[19]

Western Bahá'ís who travelled to the Holy Land in the early days of the Faith have left us these fascinating accounts of the Holy Family:

In 'Abdu'l-Bahá's household, in addition to Himself, His wife, His sister, two married daughters with husbands and children, and His two youngest daughters, there were some orphan children and widows of martyrs. Mary Lucas observed that: 'These serve in some capacity in the household, and the sentiment of love and equality in every member of this home is a living example for the world. Everything is done in the spirit of love.'

Corinne True recorded what she observed on an early pilgrimage: 'Arising early I went into the living room where the Master meets with His family every morning between six and seven o'clock. The widow of one of the martyrs sits on the floor in the Persian style and makes and serves the tea every morning . . . Having lost all of her relatives through the persecution, and Persian women having no openings for self-support, the Master took her into His household. What a wonderful household this is – over forty people living here in one home, some black, some white, Arabic, Persian, Burmanese, Italian, Russian and now English and American! Not a loud command is heard and not one word of dispute; not one word of fault-finding. Everyone goes about as if on tip toes. When they enter your room, their slippers are left before the door and they come in with stocking feet and remain standing until you invite them to sit down.[20]

3

Unity and Diversity within the Family

Roles and Functions of Individual Members

When God bestows upon us the gift of parenthood He charges us with unique and clearly-defined responsibilities. Within the Bahá'í Writings are found specific requirements for mothers, fathers, the parents jointly and their children. When each member of the family fulfils his or her God-given responsibilities the harmonious and efficient functioning of the family is ensured.

In a previous chapter the Bahá'í family was likened to the Local Spiritual Assembly. A close parallel also exists in the way in which the individuals in both institutions fulfil different responsibilities for the advancement of the whole. Within the Assembly different members have different functions. For example, the chairman chairs each meeting and ensures the standard of consultation; the chairman's guidance is deferred to in matters relating to the free and frank expression of each member or adherence to the agenda. The secretary keeps a record of each meeting and takes care of correspondence. The secretary, in consultation with the chairman, calls the meetings of the Assembly. The treasurer keeps financial records. The officers of the Assembly are elected because of their ability and experience; in their special areas they can guide and advise the Assembly but none can dictate to, or dominate, the others.

Within the family, too, we see division of roles and functions. These are due to the special abilities and experience of the members. As with the Assembly, neither partner can dominate, or dictate to, the other. The Guardian states:

> From the fact that there is no equality of functions between the sexes one should not, however, infer that either sex is inherently superior or inferior to the other, or that they are unequal in their rights.[1]

The differences in functions between husband and wife are as necessary and complementary as the functions of chairman and treasurer. However there are really very few distinctions and these few are because of the difference in the innate qualities of men and women. For example, 'Abdu'l-Bahá tells us that when the defence of the community is necessary

> . . . it is the duty of men to organize and execute such defensive measures and not the women − because their hearts are tender and they cannot endure the sight of the horror of carnage, even if it is for the sake of defence. From such and similar undertakings the women are exempt.[2]

Women have been given both physical and spiritual qualities which specifically fit them to give birth to and rear infant children. A corollary of maternity is increased physical and emotional vulnerability; the complementary role is the father's responsibility to provide for and protect the family.

Because her children are a mother's chief responsibility and because, whilst they are very young, her activities are largely centred around the home and around them, the mother is in a better situation to estimate and advise on the suitability of the home conditions as they relate to the material and spiritual progress of the child. Indeed, it is described as her unique privilege.

For this reason, it would seem that in matters of consultation to do with this aspect of family life, the mother should be considered an 'expert' and, if necessary, her opinion deferred to.

The Nature of Deference

What is meant by deference? Does it mean that the less assertive of the two partners should 'give in'? The Universal House of Justice gives the following guidance:

> There are . . . times when a wife should defer to her husband, and times when a husband should defer to his wife, but neither should ever unjustly dominate the other.[3]

Obviously, if one party is forbidden to dominate unjustly the other, there can be no room for the more assertive of the two to be the 'winner', for if one person feels a victim of injustice there can be no unity, and unity is the fundamental value to be maintained at all times. In fact, it is better for one partner, believing his or her opinion to be 'correct', to agree to a wrong decision to maintain unity than to force that opinion upon the other.

'Abdu'l-Bahá says:

> If they agree upon a subject, even though it be wrong, it is better than to disagree and be in the right, for this difference will produce the demolition of the divine foundation. Though one of the parties may be in the right and they disagree that will be the cause of a thousand wrongs, but if they agree and both parties are in the wrong, as it is in unity the truth will be revealed and the wrong made right.[4]

In our day-to-day life there are many situations in which we disagree with another's opinion but decide, upon consideration, to defer to that person. This may be because we consider that the other is more knowledgeable or experienced in the field concerned. An extreme example of this might be a brain surgeon who tells me that I have a terminal tumour when I think that I am feeling really great. If my child's teacher tells me that he is below average in mathematics, I may decide that, as the teacher is likely to have better knowledge of my child's present attainment in the field than I do, I will accept her opinion and arrange for extra tuition. Conversely, I may have reason to think that the teacher has less ability in mathematics than I and so choose not to act on her advice.

Generally speaking, it makes sense that where two people initially hold differing views, greatest consideration should be given to the most experienced or qualified of the two, or to the one who has the direct responsibility for that area. Following this, when one person's view has been wholeheartedly accepted, the partners should proceed to act in complete unity. Because family members have differing functions, each brings to consultation a different area of expertise. Also, each will have had a different experience of the subject under consideration. For individuals who are relatively new to Bahá'í consultation, these differences seem very daunting; one wonders if anything can be agreed upon. It is as if two people were to sit on either side of a teapot. One can see only a handle, while the other can see only a spout. It appears at first that something is radically wrong. Only if each person tries to see the pot from the other's unique point of view will the truth be revealed. Even then it is only a relative truth for if another person were to be looking directly down upon the teapot he would see only a sphere with two projections. Obviously we can never see exactly what another sees and it is this necessity for trust and reliance upon one another's integrity which promotes the development of unity.

The Complementary Nature of Roles within the Family

Having considered how the difference in functions of family members contributes to the general well-being of the family, we will now turn to the responsibilities in detail. In order to derive a true understanding of the matter, however, it is important to see the Writings in perspective:

The House of Justice suggests that all statements in the Holy Writings concerning specific areas of the relationship between men and women should be considered in the light of the general principle of equality between the sexes that has been authoritatively and repeatedly enunciated in the Sacred Texts. In one of His Tablets 'Abdu'l-Bahá asserts: 'In this divine age the bounties of God have encompassed the world of women. Equality of men and women, except in some negligible instances, has been fully and categorically announced. Distinctions have been utterly removed.' That men and women differ from one another in certain characteristics and functions is an inescapable fact of nature; the important thing is that 'Abdu'l-Bahá regards such inequalities as remain between the sexes as being 'negligible'.

The relationship between husband and wife must be viewed in the context of the Bahá'í ideal of family life. Bahá'u'lláh came to bring unity to the world, and a fundamental unity is that of the family. Therefore, one must believe that the Faith is intended to strengthen the family, not weaken it, and one of the keys to the strengthening of unity is loving consultation. The atmosphere within a Bahá'í family as within the community as a whole should express 'the keynote of the Cause of God' which, the beloved Guardian has stated, 'is not dictatorial authority but humble fellowship, not arbitrary power, but the spirit of frank and loving consultation.'[5]

This quotation is from the introductory paragraphs of a

message from the Universal House of Justice which considers the matter of specific functions of family members. Many of the quotations in this chapter are from this message which, because of its direct pertinence to the subject under consideration, will be quoted in its entirety. This will also enable it to be studied, and will permit the brief passages referred to later to be considered in perspective.

> A family, however, is a very special kind of 'community'. The Research Department has not come across any statements which specifically name the father as responsible for the 'security, progress and unity of the family' . . . but it can be inferred from a number of the responsibilities placed upon him, that the father can be regarded as the 'head' of the family. The members of a family all have duties and responsibilities towards one another and to the family as a whole, and these duties and responsibilities vary from member to member because of their natural relationships. The parents have the inescapable duty to educate their children – but not vice versa; the children have the duty to obey their parents – the parents do not obey the children; the mother – not the father – bears the children, nurses them in babyhood, and is thus their first educator, hence daughters have a prior right to education over sons and, as the Guardian's secretary has written on his behalf: 'The task of bringing up a Bahá'í child, as emphasized time and again in Bahá'í Writings, is the chief responsibility of the mother, whose unique privilege is indeed to create in her home such conditions as would be most conducive to both his material and spiritual welfare and advancement. The training which the child first receives through his mother constitutes the strongest foundation for his future development.' A corollary of this responsibility of the mother is her right to be supported by her husband – a husband has no explicit right to be supported by his wife. This principle of the husband's responsibility to provide for and protect the family can be seen applied also in the law of intestacy which provides that

the family's dwelling place passes, on the father's death, not
to his widow, but to his eldest son; the son at the same time
has the responsibility to care for his mother.

It is in this context of mutual and complementary duties
and responsibilities that one should read the Tablet in which
'Abdu'l-Bahá gives the following exhortation:

> 'O Handmaids of the Self-Sustaining Lord! Exert your
> efforts so that you may attain the honour and privilege
> ordained for women. Undoubtedly the greatest glory
> of women is servitude at His threshold and submissive-
> ness at His door; it is the possession of a vigilant heart,
> and praise of the incomparable God; it is heartfelt love
> towards other handmaids and spotless chastity; it is
> obedience to and consideration for their husbands and
> the education and care of their children; and it is
> tranquillity, and dignity, perseverance in the remem-
> brance of the Lord, and the utmost enkindlement and
> attraction.'

This exhortation to the utmost degree of spirituality and
self-abnegation should not be read as a legal definition
giving the husband absolute authority over his wife, for, in
a letter written to an individual believer on 22 July 1943, the
beloved Guardian's secretary wrote on his behalf:

> 'The Guardian, in his remarks . . . about parents and
> children, wives and husbands relations in America,
> meant that there is a tendency in that country for
> children to be too independent of the wishes of their
> parents and lacking in the respect due to them. Also
> wives, in some cases, have a tendency to exert an
> unjust degree of domination over their husbands
> which, of course, is not right, any more than that the
> husband should unjustly dominate his wife.'

In any group, however loving the consultation, there are
nevertheless points on which, from time to time, agreement cannot be reached. In a Spiritual Assembly this
dilemma is resolved by a majority vote. There can,

however, be no majority where only two parties are involved, as in the case of a husband and wife. There are, therefore, times when a wife should defer to her husband, and times when a husband should defer to his wife, but neither should ever unjustly dominate the other. In short, the relationship between husband and wife should be as held forth in the prayer revealed by 'Abdu'l-Bahá which is often read at Bahá'í weddings: 'Verily they are married in obedience to Thy command. Cause them to become the signs of harmony and unity till the end of time.'

These are all relationships within the family, but there is a much wider sphere of relationships between men and women than in the home, and this too we should consider in the context of Bahá'í society, not in that of past or present social norms. For example, although the mother is the first educator of the child, and the most important formative influence in his development, the father also has the responsibility of educating his children, and this responsibility is so weighty that Bahá'u'lláh has stated that a father who fails to exercise it forfeits his rights of fatherhood. Similarly, although the primary responsibility for supporting the family financially is placed upon the husband, this does not by any means imply that the place of women is confined to the home. On the contrary, 'Abdu'l-Bahá has stated:

'In this Revelation of Bahá'u'lláh, the women go neck and neck with the men. In no movement will they be left behind. Their rights with men are equal in degree. They will enter all the administrative branches of politics. They will attain in all such a degree as will be considered the very highest station of the world of humanity and will take part in all affairs.' (*Paris Talks*, p. 182.)

and again:

'So it will come to pass that when women participate fully and equally in the affairs of the world, enter confidently and capably the great arena of law and politics, war will cease . . . ' (*The Promulgation of Universal Peace*, Vol. II, p. 369.)

In the Tablet of the World, Bahá'u'lláh Himself has envisaged that women as well as men would be breadwinners in stating:

'Everyone, whether man or woman, should hand over to a trusted person a portion of what he or she earneth through trade, agriculture or other occupation, for the training and education of children, to be spent for this purpose with the knowledge of the Trustees of the House of Justice.' (*Tablets of Bahá'u'lláh*, p.90.)

A very important element in the attainment of such equality is Bahá'u'lláh's provision that boys and girls must follow essentially the same curriculum in schools.[6]

A Summary of the Roles of Father, Mother and Children

Some responsibilities of the husband and father

- the father can be regarded as the 'head' of the family[7]

- a husband has no explicit right to be supported by his wife[8]

- when the defence of the community is necessary, men, not women, must organize and execute such defensive measures, for the women are exempt[9]

- although the mother is the first educator of the child, the father also has the responsibility of educating his children, and the father who fails to exercise it forfeits his rights of fatherhood.[10] (This is a very significant statement for it asserts that the rights of fatherhood are not dependent upon blood relationship but upon taking the responsibility for the education of the children, a concept totally foreign to popular attitudes towards fatherhood.)

- the husband has the primary responsibility for supporting the family financially[11]

Some responsibilities of the wife and mother

- the task of bringing up a Bahá'í child is the chief responsibility of the mother[12]

- it is '. . . the mother, whose unique privilege is indeed to create in her home such conditions as would be most conducive to both his [the child's] material and spiritual welfare and advancement'[13]

- mothers 'determine the happiness, the future greatness, the courteous ways and learning and judgement, the understanding and faith of their little ones'[14]

- it is the mother's right to be supported by her husband – a husband has no explicit right to be supported by his wife[15]

- every man and woman should hand over to a trusted person a portion of what he or she earns for the training and education of children[16]

Some responsibilities of the children

(Please note that in this context 'children' does not always refer to those who have not yet attained the age of maturity, but rather describes how we should all relate to our parents)

- children have the duty to obey their parents[17]

- after the recognition of the Oneness of God, the most important of all duties is to have due regard for the rights of one's parents[18]

- children 'must show forth charity and beneficence, and must implore pardon and forgiveness for their parents'[19]

- fathers and mothers are worthy of esteem and it is necessary for children to secure their good pleasure[20]

- a child ought, in return for the love and kindness shown by his father, to give to the poor for his sake[21]

- the consent of all living parents is required for a Bahá'í marriage[22]

- the law of intestacy provides that the family's dwelling place passes, on the father's death, to his eldest son; the son at the same time has the responsibility to care for his mother.[23]

These are some of the specific responsibilities of individual family members, responsibilities which, when applied in the light of the Bahá'í principles, will strengthen the family and enhance its unity. They require thoughtful deliberation in order to achieve this benefit, for a right principle applied in a wrong way can actually be a source of harm. The actual forms or practical applications of each will be as many and varied as the families who apply them, and will be decided through harmonious consultation. Because the circumstances within the family are subject to change from time to time, so must the application of these responsibilities be reconsidered and reapplied when necessary. 'Abdu'l-Bahá described the family bond as follows:

According to the teachings of Bahá'u'lláh the family, being a human unit, must be educated according to the rules of sanctity. All the virtues must be taught the family. The integrity of the family bond must be constantly considered, and the rights of the individual members must not be transgressed. The rights of the son, the father, the mother – none of them must be transgressed, none of them must be arbitrary. Just as the son has certain obligations to his father, the father, likewise, has certain obligations to his son. The mother, the sister and other members of the household have their certain prerogatives. All these rights and prerogatives must be conserved, yet the unity of the family must be sustained. The injury of one shall be considered the injury of all; the comfort of each the comfort of all; the honour of one, the honour of all.[24]

4

Implementing the Equality of Men and Women

The Bahá'í family of our time must face with determination, perseverance and assurance one of the most momentous and profound challenges imaginable. Its place is at the forefront of a revolution in human relationships unknown in the entire history of humankind, in the leading ranks of those whose task it is to embark upon a long, gradual and irreversible process: implementing the equality of men and women.

This new paradigm in human relationships is of special significance to the family because it is here that we experience the most sustained and intimate interface of male/female relationships from our earliest, most impressionable years. It requires husbands and wives to revolutionize ancient roles and attitudes, to tear down traditional patterns of dominance and submission and yet to achieve this in such a way that, rather than setting the stage for a battle of wills, the foundation is laid for such unity and harmony as will make them even as a single soul. Developing from infancy in such an atmosphere of unity and harmony, sisters and brothers will view one another as true equals and will learn the lessons of mutual cooperation, support and respect, taking as an enduring example the relationships portrayed daily by their parents.

Until this era, the order and functioning of the family, as for the community and the nation, was a reflection of the inferior role of women. The dominance of the male meant also a predominance of the qualities in which men are strong, as 'Abdu'l-Bahá has indicated:

> The world in the past has been ruled by force, and man has dominated over woman by reason of his more forceful and aggressive qualities both of body and mind. But the balance is already shifting – force is losing its weight, and mental alertness, intuition, and the spiritual qualities of love and service, in which woman is strong, are gaining ascendancy. Hence the new age will be an age less masculine, and more permeated with the feminine ideals – or, to speak more exactly, will be an age in which the masculine and feminine elements of civilization will be more evenly balanced.[1]

Such a dramatic reversal away from the timeworn values of humankind towards this new balance of qualities has sweeping ramifications, both now and for the future. It affects each of us, male and female, very personally, as we are freed from traditional sex-role stereotypes which overemphasize some of our personal qualities whilst suppressing others. Free of such restraint, we are able to come to know our own selves in the infinite variety and richness of our creation, to discover undreamed-of depths, to educate and refine the gems which we find deposited by God in our innermost souls, and to offer them in the service of mankind.

It is impossible to predict, at this dawntime in the new age of human relationships, all those fruits which may be born in the future. However, we may be sure that if the remarkable march of progress in past civilizations was achieved largely by the endeavours of only half of humankind, then the future will be spectacular. Not only will it be enriched as a result of enlisting the abilities, energy and vision of a previously untapped force, but the spiritual power resulting from working in unity and cooperation will lend enormous energy and impetus to the affairs of humanity. These arguments were first stated by 'Abdu'l-Bahá:

> Until womankind reaches the same degree as man, until she enjoys the same arena of activity, extraordinary attainment for humanity will not be realized; humanity cannot wing its way to heights of real attainment. When the two wings or parts become equivalent in strength, enjoying the same prerogatives, the flight of man will be exceedingly lofty and extraordinary. Therefore, woman must receive the same education as man and all inequality be adjusted. Thus, imbued with the same virtues as man, rising through all the degrees of human attainment, women will become the peers of men, and until this equality is established, true progress and attainment for the human race will not be facilitated.
>
> The evident reasons underlying this are as follows: Woman by nature is opposed to war; she is an advocate of peace. Children are reared and brought up by the mothers who give them the first principles of education and labour assiduously in their behalf. Consider, for instance, a mother who has tenderly reared a son for twenty years to the age of maturity. Surely she will not consent to having that son torn asunder and killed in the field of battle. Therefore, as woman advances toward the degree of man in power and privilege, with the right of vote and control in human government, most assuredly war will cease; for woman is naturally the most devoted and staunch advocate of international peace.[2]

There are several results of the establishment of equality between men and women about which we may be sure. The true emancipation of women will be the greatest factor in the establishment of world peace. It will also allow men to achieve a greatness denied them in the past because they were raised and first educated by a deficient womankind. Humanity as a whole will benefit from receiving wise and thorough education during the most crucial formative years as a result of competent and knowledgeable mothering. When fully one half of the world's population, previously denied any significant contribution to civilization outside the circle of family and home, becomes educated and fully participating, humanity will be doubly enriched. Women, working in unity and concord, will be enabled to promote and implement Bahá'í teachings with knowledge, power, confidence and support, thus hastening the advent of the Golden Age of the Faith, the Kingdom of God on earth. So long as we delay in implementing the principle of the equality of men and women, for so long do we prevent ourselves from experiencing this revolutionary transformation in the affairs of a sorry and suffering humanity.

In order to implement such a change, it is helpful to understand the background to what is often erroneously thought of as a uniquely modern concept and a recent capacity. We need to recognize and understand the relative nature of the difference in male and female qualities and to become familiar with the roles expected of women, as delineated in the Bahá'í Writings.

It is not correct to assume that women achieved the capacity for equality only in the Dispensation of Bahá'u'lláh. The Bahá'í Writings are quite emphatic that women have always possessed this capacity but state that the realization of it was denied through lack of opportunity and education. Ours is not the first age in history to witness movements for equality. Neither are the women of this age the first to demonstrate their innate capacity. 'Abdu'l-Bahá states that in past ages some women have risen in the affairs of nations and eclipsed the efforts of men in their accomplish-ments. Proof of such capacity in bygone times may be seen in the lives of women such as Sarah, Mary Magdalene,

Fatimih and Ṭáhirih. These outstanding women surpassed the men of their times and rendered services of imperishable glory to the Cause of God. However, in this day, Bahá'u'lláh has given a special impetus by greatly strengthening the cause of women.

Acceptance of the principle of the equality of women is only the first step, a statement that one has recognized the truth of this tenet. It is a dangerous illusion to believe that the Bahá'í Faith has perfected the application of equality, or that any of us, whether man or woman, fully embodies such a belief in our lives. Even the most enlightened Bahá'í in this day is just glimpsing the first light of true equality because, as with every other principle of our Faith, the understanding and application of truth is progressive.

The Responsibilities of Women

We should not suppose that since Bahá'u'lláh has enunciated this principle, suddenly all women have attained to true equality and immediately deserve equal qualifications and status with men. In *Paris Talks*, it is recorded that 'Abdu'l-Bahá has said, 'It is not to be denied that in various directions woman at present is more backward than man, also that this temporary inferiority is due to the lack of educational opportunity.'[3] Therefore, it is apparent that until such inequality has been overcome, women cannot demonstrate their true potential:

> Woman must endeavour then to attain greater perfection, to be man's equal in every respect, to make progress in all in which she has been backward, so that man will be compelled to acknowledge her equality of capacity and attainment.[4]

In the Bahá'í teachings, women are enjoined to 'endeavour' and to 'strive', to 'progress' and to 'attain', to 'demonstrate' and to 'prove'. This requires each woman –

through personal meditation, in loving consultation with her husband, if she has one, in groups with other women, and in the organized women's meetings which must be established in every community – to plan for and cultivate personal growth, to seek to identify the areas in which she is indeed deficient, to remedy them and to acquire new skills and abilities. This may be a very painful process. It involves bringing oneself to account with scrupulous honesty, freely acknowledging any inferiority of attainment, knowledge and accomplishment, but all this with a deep inner conviction of self-worth, of determination and of ultimate triumph. This is in truth the field of the pioneer. We are among the first women in the history of the planet to take these early steps in revolutionizing the life of all humankind, to light the way for women to become such fluent, eloquent and radiant teachers that they will join the ranks of the leaders of the learned. We can be assured that the fruits of our efforts will be borne down through the ages, for 'Abdu'l-Bahá has said:

> Women must make the greatest effort to acquire spiritual power and to increase in the virtue of wisdom and holiness until their enlightenment and striving succeeds in bringing about the unity of mankind. They must work with a burning enthusiasm to spread the Teaching of Bahá'u'lláh among the peoples, so that the radiant light of the Divine Bounty may envelop the souls of all the nations of the world![5]

'Abdu'l-Bahá has stated that not only must women attain such power, but they must demonstrate it before the eyes of others who would challenge their true capacity. He further states that women must become proficient in the arts and sciences, and especially devote their energies and abilities to the industrial and agricultural sciences, seeking to give assistance where it is most needed; this will ensure recognition of equality in social and economic affairs.

They should, through teaching and the active moral support they give to every movement directed towards peace, seek to exert a strong influence on public opinion and especially on the minds of other women – to be educators and role models – until such a conscious and overwhelming mass of public opinion against war is formed that there can be no war.

In teaching the Faith, women must strive to perfect their knowledge of divine realities, so that they may take a position among the learned, will each have a fluent tongue and eloquent speech. Women must form gatherings wherein they will develop such ability, will gain mastery in demonstrating reasons and proofs and in quoting verses and traditions . . . 'so that all the homes of the loved ones will be converted into gathering places for lessons on teaching the Cause'.[6]

These, then, are the criteria for women seeking to attain true equality, to realize the noble mission which, in this Dispensation, has been clearly set before them. Each woman must resolve to accept these as personal goals, to evaluate her present attainment and to seek ways, both as an individual and working in groups, whereby the goals may be met. A following chapter will give consideration to goal-setting and achievement.

The Responsibilities of Men

Men, too, have a responsibility in establishing the equality of men and women. Husbands must be the 'helpmeets' of wives, a role defined in the *Collins Dictionary* as 'a less common word for helpmate', 'a companion and helper, esp. a wife'. This definition amply demonstrates how entrenched is the attitude that the role of wives is to support their husbands and not vice versa. Other descriptions of the function of a helpmeet include aide, ally, colleague, partner, supporter and facilitator. It is important for men to become actively involved in and committed to the cause of equality. In many cases the power to change is still vested in the control of men, and this is a worthy way of acknowledging their debt of gratitude to the countless women of ages past who, arising to fulfil their traditional role of helpmeet, enabled men to achieve their present degree of accomplishment.

Men can work towards the goal of equality on many sides – in their personal attitudes, in their marriages, in Bahá'í community life and in the larger sphere of human society through their educative influence within their occupations, and in any clubs, sporting or cultural groups to which they may belong.

In order to change personal attitudes – those thoughts of the inner man which may be known only to the individual and to God – one must pray, meditate and become so informed about the subject that knowledge, coupled with true commitment, personal will and volition, will gradually produce changes in outward behaviour and action. Oppressive personal attitudes cannot be legislated against in the same sweeping way in which, for example, a country can give women the right to vote. Men must overcome mannerisms and habits which reinforce negative views of women. This includes refraining from language which denigrates women – for example the use of terms such as 'girl', 'baby', or 'chick' which, whilst perhaps not intended to offend, nonetheless present images of cuteness, helplessness and weakness, and suggest that these are attractive, ideal, feminine qualities. Rather, we must seek to use terms which convey respect, regard and esteem for the equal capacity and accomplishments of women. We must refrain from using jokes, innuendoes and terms of speech which highlight the weak or sexual nature of women and girls, and reject magazines and other entertainments which

promote denigrating attitudes. The man who refrains
from such behaviour, whilst exemplifying friendly and
courteous attitudes to those with whom he associates in
every sphere of his life, is a beacon of light whose
influence will spread. Not only is he setting an example
for other men, but his respectful treatment of women will
encourage them to greater personal confidence and progress.
'Abdu'l-Bahá states:

> In brief, the assumption of superiority by man will continue
> to be depressing to the ambition of woman, as if her
> attainment to equality was creationally impossible; woman's
> aspiration toward advancement will be checked by it, and
> she will gradually become hopeless. On the contrary, we
> must declare that her capacity is equal, even greater than
> man's. This will inspire her with hope and ambition, and
> her susceptibilities for advancement will continually increase.
> She must not be told and taught that she is weaker and
> inferior in capacity and qualification.[7]

Most importantly, the attitudes and practices of fathers
can set an extremely positive example to their children.
Thus sons and daughters will grow up embodying the
attitudes of both father and mother which attest to the
equal rights, opportunities, privileges and capacity of
women.

Husbands must consult with wives as to the ordering
and administering of all household affairs, the division of
responsibility in respect of these tasks, the roles of each
partner in respect of breadwinning, and the education of
the children. In all of these, as we have seen, *both* partners
have a responsibility, to one degree or another. To this
end each must have a basic knowledge of the Bahá'í
Writings on the subject so that their decisions reflect
divine wisdom rather than ignorance or prejudice. An
important means of education is the institution of community women's meetings for here women will become

informed of the Bahá'í teachings, will become learned and will, with fluency and eloquence, spread this knowledge throughout the world. The men of a Bahá'í community can do much to ensure the establishment of such programmes – to make them a priority in planning, to champion their aims and to enable the fullest attendance possible amongst the women of the community, including planning for such practical issues as the care of young children so that mothers may be free to attend.

When men own the equality of women there will be no need for them to struggle for their rights![8]

As was considered in a previous chapter, equality does not mean sameness. In addition to having distinct roles and responsibilities in some areas of life, the sexes also possess spiritual qualities in different degrees. The emphasis here is of degree: all are made in the image of God and all potentially possess each of the qualities of the spirit. However, in keeping with our differing roles, we each possess these qualities to greater or less degrees.

Some Qualities of Men

The world in the past has been ruled by force, and man has dominated over woman by reason of his more forceful and aggressive qualities both of body and mind.[9]

. . . man is more inclined to war than woman . . .[10]

'. . . women have assumed the attributes of men [which are] steadfastness in the Cause of God . . . heroism and might . . .'[11]

Some Qualities of Women

In some respects woman is superior to man. She is more tender-hearted, more receptive, her intuition is more intense.[12]

. . . mental alertness, intuition, and the spiritual qualities of love and service, in which woman is strong . . . [13]

Woman by nature is opposed to war; she is an advocate of peace . . . woman is naturally the most devoted and staunch advocate of international peace. [14]

. . . their hearts are tender and they cannot endure the sight of the horror of carnage . . . [15]

. . . as regards tenderness of heart and the abundance of mercy and sympathy ye are superior. [16]

. . . women are most capable and efficient . . . their hearts are more tender and susceptible than the hearts of men . . . they are more philanthropic and responsive toward the needy and suffering . . . they are inflexibly opposed to war and are lovers of peace. [17]

In some respects, women have astonishing capacities; they hasten in their attraction to God, and are intense in their fiery ardour for Him. [18]

The woman is indeed of the greater importance to the race. She has the greater burden and the greater work . . . The woman has greater moral courage than the man; she has also special gifts which enable her to govern in moments of danger and crisis. [19]

Again it should be emphasized that these particular strengths of women must be viewed in light of the understanding that neither sex has exclusive qualities, that it is the degree of a quality that is significant. However, it is true that men and women have unique roles which draw upon those qualities in which they are often particularly strong; so, for example, the woman is strong in those qualities which are necessary to bear, nurture and raise infants, but unique in her physical abilities to do so.

Division of Tasks within the Family

An earlier chapter considered the functions and responsibilities of husband and wife in terms of general Bahá'í principles. It is valuable also to consider the practical division of roles within the family, particularly with a view to determining whether the distribution of tasks reflects the most equitable and beneficial use of capacity and resources, allows for the flexibility necessary to any organic, changing and evolving structure, and is productive of the equality of men and women. This section also gives consideration to the needs of those whose work is centred on the home – particularly mothers and homemakers – and the role of both stipendiary and unpaid work. This last includes those who are fortunate enough to give a great deal of their time to the administrative, service and teaching fields of the Faith. The Universal House of Justice validates such occupations as being of benefit to mankind and therefore as constituting 'work'. It also clarifies how a family may determine the relative amounts of time which the mother may spend both within and without the home, describes the overlapping of roles in the areas of bread-winning and education, advocates flexibility and provision for necessary adjustments, and emphasizes that arrangements made by the family must provide for the full and equal participation of the wife in the affairs of the world.

> You ask about the admonition that everyone must work, and want to know if this means that you, a wife and mother, must work for a livelihood as your husband does. We are requested to enclose for your perusal an excerpt, 'The twelfth Glad-Tidings', from Bahá'u'lláh's 'Tablet of Bishárát'. You will see that the directive is for the friends to be engaged in an occupation which will be of benefit to mankind. Homemaking is a highly honourable and responsible work of fundamental importance for mankind.[20]

With regard to your question whether mothers should work outside the home, it is helpful to consider the matter from the perspective of the concept of a Bahá'í family. This concept is based on the principle that the man has primary responsibility for the financial support of the family, and the woman is the chief and primary educator of the children. This by no means implies that these functions are inflexibly fixed and cannot be changed and adjusted to suit particular family situations, nor does it mean that the place of the woman is confined to the home. Rather, while primary responsibility is assigned, it is anticipated that fathers would play a significant role in the education of the children and women could also be breadwinners. As you rightly indicated, 'Abdu'l-Bahá encouraged women to 'participate fully and equally in the affairs of the world'.

In relation to your specific queries, the decision concerning the amount of time a mother may spend in working outside the home depends on circumstances existing within the home, which may vary from time to time. Family consultation will help to provide the answers.[21]

The status and value accorded to wives, by their own selves as well as by their husbands, can also be gauged by observation of roles. The following questions are intended to provoke thought. They are in no way a specific indicator of inequality for, as discussed in an earlier chapter, it may be the informed preference of the partners to fulfil many traditional roles. The point to consider here is whether roles within the family are a product of blind imitation or whether they have been determined through consultation and make the best use of strengths and resources, while allowing for flexibility, growth and progress.

Consideration of Equality in General Family Organization

- Is responsibility for matters pertaining to property, finances, utilities and household services, insurance and local or national government issues given to the husband? There is not necessarily any problem with such an arrangement. However, there is concern if any of the following apply:

    1. The role was simply assumed by the husband in the absence of any joint consultation because of traditional role models. There is equally a problem if the wife assumed the same role without consultation. To be the most effective, all matters should be the result of consultation.

    2. The role was assumed by the husband as the wife did not have the education and skills to deal with these matters. Here is an inequality due to lack of education and one which can and should be remedied. Wives need to take an educated role in consultation so that decision-making reflects informed opinions. Also, wives often live longer than their husbands and a bereavement is quite traumatic in itself, without the aggravation of the wife suddenly finding herself solely responsible for financial and other business affairs of which she is both ignorant and incapable of managing.

    3. The partner not responsible for these matters is not given a regular report to enable him or her to have a general grasp of the on-going situation. In most types of social organization, there is provision for the individual responsible for specialized areas, i.e. the treasurer, to make regular reports so that others may be informed and take this knowledge

into account in decision-making. Certainly the family should take advantage of the natural abilities and inclinations of each member in allocating responsibility but it is usually wise to ensure some regular report-back system so that the general state of affairs is familiar to others.

- Are property ownership papers in the names of both parties?

- Do both partners have the same opportunity to advance in their occupations, to avail themselves of secondary or tertiary education, to gain necessary qualifications?

- Will they each receive the necessary practical support and resources to achieve this?

- If one partner has less education than the other, is some compensation being made to address this inequality?

- Do both partners have equal access to trade and professional magazines pertaining to their fields so that they may be kept informed of advances, find stimulation and advice and extend their knowledge?

- Do both partners have equitable access to personal spending money?

- Are both expected to be accountable to the same degree for any money spent as a result of their occupations – for example, entertaining associates, purchasing essential work items, paying registration fees for seminars and conferences, purchasing suitable clothing and accessories such as briefcases or filing systems, staying in paid accommodation if necessary?

- Who is expected to provide the care for ill children or dependent relatives?

- Who writes to family and friends?

- Who remembers special occasions and selects, wraps and sends gifts?

- Who prepares for family holidays? Who makes the practical arrangements – who packs the clothes?

- Who buys the family's provisions, cooks, cleans, mends, repairs, recycles, renovates, maintains, provides transport, listens, gives first aid, attends school meetings and organizes fund raising events?

When the Wife Works Largely in the Home

- Is the value of women's magazines appreciated as much as those pertaining to the career needs of men? (Many are quality productions which contain valuable information on a variety of subjects such as nutrition, health, care of children, household management, women's issues, ideas and information on career options, job-sharing and professional advice pertinent to the needs of women striving to achieve equality in their fields.)

- Do both partners have the same access to holidays entirely free from their main occupations, including breaks away from child-rearing or from household management and cooking when these are the primary occupations.

- Do both partners have equal access to on-going education in their chosen fields, including household management and child education if these are primary responsibilities?

- Are the occupations of mother or household manager given such resources as reflect the value placed upon them by 'Abdu'l-Bahá? (This may be indicated by comparing whether both partners have the same access to resources. Those employed outside the home may take for granted such benefits as the ability to take sick leave entirely away from the job – a benefit not readily available to those rearing small children in the home – the provision of a personal workspace with stationery and equipment supplied, and set lunch hours which can be taken away from the workplace. Such provisions may also be of great advantage to the worker in the home.)

- Most occupations acknowledge achievement, effort, excellence, rank and status in some way – by pay rises; bonuses; personal offices complete with name plate; newer, larger and more plentiful office furniture; personal business cards; job titles indicating seniority; parking spaces; company cars; and executive privileges. These are all the trappings which indicate success in the outside world. Whilst some of these examples are in reality shallow and insubstantial, they raise the question as to the rewards given to those who work in the home. Bahá'í's believe that reward and punishment are essential, that they train all of us. It has been claimed that ideally virtue is its own reward and the knowledge of a job well done is reward in itself. Nonetheless, 'Abdu'l-Bahá spoke of the value of praise and encouragement. What provision does the family make to reward the person in the home, to praise, encourage, acknowledge and indicate value?

- Do family roles and responsibilities allow for flexibility? (The nature of the family changes with the arrival of another child or with the growing independence of existing children. Similarly, the relative dependence of children upon the mother or father increases or decreases. The mother's or father's time commitments to the balance of work within and without the home must change and, consequently, so may the role of breadwinner. This may be variously shared by the marriage partners or may be the sole responsibility of only one partner, as circumstances allow.)

The Requirements of the Community

The Bahá'í Writings clearly delineate those factors which are the foundation of equality. They include equality of rights, privileges, development, opportunities, advancement, education, prerogatives, qualification and power afforded through the right to vote and through equal opportunity for participation and control in human government, law and all the administrative branches of politics. In brief, women should have the same arena of activity as men.

Upon consideration, it may be found that our Bahá'í communities and families are just putting into place the first foundation stones of such equality. These may consist of no more than a general raising of consciousness about the subject, through deepenings and study classes, or perhaps only through individuals discussing the subject amongst themselves informally. These are important first steps, but there is much to be done. When we delay the progress of this cause, we delay the advent of world peace, prolong the suffering of humankind and add to the burden which must eventually be shouldered by our children and our children's children.

The current status of women can be gauged by examining the roles which are played in Bahá'í community life. Does the community continue to give the prominent positions within the community to men? For example, are the roles of chairman and treasurer of Assemblies or committees generally filled by men? Are introductions, speeches and reports given by men? Is the community's delegate to Annual Convention usually male? Is the role of secretary usually filled by a woman? Is it men whose voices and opinions predominate in consultation? Are roles which require preparation of food, serving of food, caring for children and tidying, cleaning and washing up, usually carried out by women? Are repetitive, low-profile jobs and communications, such as phoning around the community and the preparation and distribution of news-letters, routinely done by women? Not only do these questions highlight the present status of women within a community, but they also give an indication as to how sex roles within the Faith are perceived by the non-Bahá'í public who may see a hypocritical discrepancy between our words and our deeds.

If many of the questions above can be answered in the affirmative, then one of two situations probably exists. It may occasionally be the case that the women of that particular community have not acquired equal capacity to fulfil the roles now taken by men. If this is so, then the community must assume responsibility for changing such a state of affairs, through provision of deepenings, training programmes or other methods which will ensure that every woman has the education, the means and the support to overcome her deficiencies and to acquire new skills. Of course, it must be acknowledged that, even with the best training in the world, not every woman can become an excellent speaker, just as every man cannot become an excellent cook. (Equally, not every man is an excellent speaker, nor is every woman an excellent cook.) However, until equal education and opportunities are provided, it is impossible to anticipate just what talents and capacities are waiting to be discovered. Unfortunately, it may also be the case that women are given such narrow roles in the Bahá'í community because of prejudice and continuing patterns of male domination. Thus, even though women may possess as much, or even more, ability than others, some people remain blind to it or prefer the personal advantages of the status quo. Communities where either of the foregoing cases exist are failing to provide the only remedies for inequality: in the first instance, their women members lack education; in the second instance, opportunity. 'Abdu'l-Bahá has stated:

> Until the reality of equality between man and woman is fully established and attained, the highest social development of mankind is not possible. Even granted that woman is inferior to man in some degree of capacity or accomplishment, this or any other distinction would continue to be productive of discord and trouble. The only remedy is education, opportunity; for equality means equal qualification . . .
>
> And let it be known once more that until woman and man recognize and realize equality, social and political progress here or anywhere will not be possible.[22]

Although attainment of equality depends upon the personal volition and determination of the individual woman to begin a process of personal growth, the community can emphasize the necessity of such a process, can implement programmes and provide practical assistance. A goal of the Five Year Plan was that 80 National Spiritual Assemblies would organize Bahá'í activities for women. During International Women's Year (1975) the Bahá'ís were asked to initiate and implement such programmes as would stimulate and promote the full and equal participation of women in all aspects of Bahá'í community life, so that through their accomplishments the friends would demonstrate the distinction of the Cause of God in this field of human endeavour. The Naw-Rúz Message of 1979 from the Universal House of Justice required communities to encourage Bahá'í women to exercise to the full their privileges and responsibilities in the work of the community, and in a letter to all National Assemblies, dated 23 January 1985, both local and national Bahá'í communities were asked to sponsor a wide range of activities designed to engage the attention of people from all walks of life in topics relevant to peace, including the role of women.

Communities who responded to these calls were laying the vital foundations of equality; those who did not may even now be reaping the consequences of their failure. The wider Bahá'í community is still called upon to contribute to the establishment of this principle in many ways on many levels. For example, on the world scene, the establishment of literacy training for women and girls was a global priority of the Bahá'í International Community Six Year Development Plan (1986–92). Also required is the sustained production and distribution of compilations of Bahá'í Writings on the equality of men and women, and of tapes, papers and books, including biographies of Bahá'í women, which will educate, inform and inspire.

It should not be assumed that the most impressive instances of the pursuit of equality are to be found in the Western world and that there is nothing to be learned from less developed or less privileged countries – the nations of the 'third world'. In reality, the activities and results of countries such as Kenya, Zaire, India and Panama are an example to the world. Projects aimed at literacy, training in health, crafts and agriculture, at solving family and community problems, and empowerment through spiritual principles are producing gratifying results. A series of mothers' booklets developed in Kenya in support of these programmes has been shared with Bahá'í communities around the world, and the booklets are currently being translated into 26 languages. Other projects within these national Bahá'í communities are serving to tear down ancient practices which deny women equality such as dowries, which discriminate against women, and the caste system. This is truly pioneering work.

The future must see changes in traditional social structures and facilities. Presently the world at large is taking the lead in implementing necessary advances, but as our numbers increase, as our resources and maturity allow, the Bahá'í community or individuals within that community are spearheading change which is in accord with our beliefs. This requires individual Bahá'ís who have influence to initiate such changes in their workplaces or social spheres as will promote equal participation and will be supportive of increasing flexibility in family structures. As a result of increasing public acceptance and support of adaptations such as job-sharing, glide time, split shifts, shorter working days and alternating child-rearing/breadwinning tasks between marriage partners, mothers will be enabled to be both child-rearers and breadwinners, and to contribute their abilities and influence for the benefit of society. Other possible scenarios include a return to living in extended family groups which enlist the support of youth and the elderly, family members who are not often offered the opportunity of providing a significant role in child-rearing. The vast expansion in communications systems taking place now and in future decades will allow more people to work from home: the increasing use of computers, fax machines and so on will decrease the need for co-workers to be confined to one centralized building, thus providing greater flexibility in working arrangements and places of work. Bahá'í communities with the necessary resources, size and maturity may well provide high-quality pre-school services.

In support of the empowerment of women, communities must become committed to increasing the number of women appointed to those committees and boards within the Faith that have the functions of advising, executing and governing. They must also be committed to increasing the participation of women in all community consultations by which plans and decisions are made, in order to benefit to the fullest from their qualities, abilities and influence. Although the Bahá'í elective process denies any form of electioneering, nevertheless communities may be made aware that the number of women elected to such positions is crucial to achieving unity and progress. If, upon consideration, a community finds that such a shortfall in the equal contribution of women exists, they must consider the remedy. If it is found that the disproportionately small number of elected women is due to lack of education and opportunity, then this situation must be remedied in one way. If the reason is prejudice towards the demonstrated capacity of women, another solution must be found. 'Abdu'l-Bahá states:

> From the beginning of existence until the present day, in any of the past cycles and dispensations, no assemblies for women have ever been established and classes for the purpose of spreading the teachings were never held by them. This is one of the characteristics of this glorious Dispensation and this great century. Ye should, most certainly, strive to perfect this assemblage and increase your knowledge of the realities of heavenly mysteries, so that, God willing, in a short time, women will become the same as men; they will take a leading position amongst the learned, will each have a fluent tongue and eloquent speech, and shine like unto lamps of guidance throughout the world.[23]

Widespread educational opportunities are vital for teaching equality of the sexes as a fundamental spiritual principle. We must be actively involved in advocating, and practically facilitating, the education and advancement of women and girls and in winning the support of men for this principle. Communities must have as a goal the promotion of equal participation by women in every sphere of community life, welcoming women into all types of decision-making, and generating and sustaining active grassroots participation. They must seek to foster in women a new sense of confidence in their capacities and worth, to provide practical assistance by improving the resources available to women and to provide well-planned programmes for mothers. The Universal House of Justice wrote:

> The principle of the quality between women and men, like the other teachings of the Faith, can be effectively and universally established among the friends when it is pursued in conjunction with all the other aspects of Bahá'í life. Change is an evolutionary process requiring patience with one's self and others, loving education and the passage of time as the believers deepen their knowledge of the principles of the Faith, gradually discard long-held traditional attitudes and progressively conform their lives to the unifying teachings of the Cause. [24]

5

Families in Transition

The Nature of Change

> Man is progressive; nature is stationary, without the power of progression or retrogression. Man is endowed with ideal virtues, for example intellection, volition . . . These are powers whereby man is differentiated and distinguished from all other forms of life.
>
> 'Abdu'l-Bahá[1]

We live in a time of greater change than the world has ever known. On the one hand humanity is experiencing great suffering and adversity; on the other we see amazing progress, wonderful inventions, new solutions to ancient problems and, most glorious of all, the growing strength and influence of the Bahá'í Faith with its blueprint for a new global society that will usher in the Kingdom of God on earth. And here we stand, the generation of the half-light, poised at the juncture which marks the end of an old order and the birth of a new one, with a task before us which is at once a great privilege and extremely formidable: to be the instruments of a revolution in the life of all humankind.

There are two types of change which must concern us. The first is change from without, brought upon us by the conditions of the outer world. It is inevitable that Bahá'í families will, to one extent or another, become caught up in the sufferings of our fellow humans. Hardships, often unforeseeable, may need to be faced – illness, poverty, unemployment, bereavement and so forth. Other challenges will arise as a natural consequence of the cycles of birth, growth and maturity which see the children grow up and eventually leave the family home to establish their own, separate cycles whilst the parents adjust to new roles and relationships. Whatever the nature of the tests and trials which we may experience, the purpose is the same: lovingly to educate and guide us to greater heights of knowledge, achievement and success.

The second type of change will affect us from within. Because this is a new age, old models of family life are no longer workable. As a result of working together in unity and learning the lessons born of our adversities, we have the opportunity to be innovators and trailblazers as we pioneer the creation of new models in human relationships. The great challenge which we must face as Bahá'ís is also the cause of our distinction and honour: that we, out of all humanity, have been chosen to bring about the changes that will usher in the Day of God. In order to fulfil this destiny, we need to become familiar with Bahá'í principles and practices that must be progressively developed to bring about this change, to acquire a vision of the part which marriages and families are destined to play in the future. We also need to consider how we can make our families strong and well-prepared to pass safely and successfully through this time of transition. These are some of the subjects which will be considered in this chapter.

Positive Attitudes to Change

   . . . man will have always to toil in order to earn his living. Effort is an inseparable part of man's life. It may take different forms with the changing conditions of the world, but it will be always present as a necessary element in our earthly existence. Life is after all a struggle. Progress is attained through struggle, and without such a struggle life ceases to have a meaning; it becomes even extinct. The progress of machinery has not made effort unnecessary. It has given it a new form, a new outlet.

Shoghi Effendi[2]

The life of all people is, and will remain, subject to struggle, to change and ultimately to progress. Therefore, for marriages or families to expect a continuing state of ease and composure is unrealistic. When it is understood that struggle is really just the forerunner of positive states of growth and progress, when yet again, rough billows toss the surface of the sea of life, one need no longer despair or simply imagine that a time must eventually come when the storms will all have passed and the surface will be finally still. Instead, through knowledge, faith and steadfastness, we can attain a condition in which, though the storms of life may surge on the surface, the inner depths of our being remain still and calm. Because marriages and families are not static but in a continual stage of transition, we need to implement strategies which allow us to be positive and effective, to anticipate change where possible and to set healthy, constructive directions for growth.

This is the attitude taken by the gardener. No matter how pleased he may be with the blossoms and fruit of the present season, he knows better than to expect them to last forever. Neither does he expect that any effort on his part can prolong that condition past its appointed time. The blossoms, fruit and leaves must inevitably wither and die and the plant be left to weather the storms and gales of the winter season. Then gales will cause the root system to push itself further into the soil in readiness to support even greater growth in the seasons to come, and enabling the moisture of the rainstorms to be drawn up by the plant through the searing heat of summer. New growth will begin, requiring careful staking and training in order for the plant to grow in the most desirable form. In reality, the death of the outer form, the end of fruitfulness, the drawing to a close of a cycle, the gales and rainstorms, the staking and pruning, are no calamity but the necessary prelude to a yet greater harvest.

Preparation for Change

As we have seen, preparation and planning are essential if families and marriages are to respond to both anticipated and unforeseen changes in the most positive and constructive ways. In addition to coping with changes which happen to us from without, how do we, ourselves, actually initiate change, the sort of inner change which will help us to evolve new models of marriage and family?

Because, as Bahá'u'lláh has stated, the reality of man is his thought, the first change we must bring about is changing the way we think. This means that we need to overcome and eliminate old patterns of thought which tie us to old ways of doing things, old expectations of what our roles are, old attitudes in relation to one another. Every 'old' thought ties us into a preconceived idea about Bahá'í marriage and family life and prevents us from growing in a 'new' way. We need to free ourselves of thoughts that limit us and, in their place, put thoughts that are global, progressive, unifying, constructive: in other words, we need to think as Bahá'ís.

Our Relationship to God

Of all the relationships which we may form, the greatest is

our relationship with our Creator. It is this primary relationship which is the source and the purpose of all others, for all humanity has been created to know and worship God. The bedrock upon which all lesser relationships depend is the knowledge and implementaion of God's purpose for humankind in this day.

One of the greatest limitations which afflicts us is ignorance. When we are ignorant, we can have no real understanding of the reason for our existence, of the purpose to which our lives should be devoted, of the rules and guidelines by which we may live happily and with purpose. It is only by observing the laws, ordinances and principles given to humankind through God's Manifestation that we can understand the true purpose of our existence. This knowledge helps us to adjust our personal and family life so as to be in harmony with the laws of a creation with which we interact in a mode of constant change and transition. Such knowledge enables us to become free of past limitations and makes us ready to play our part in carrying forward an ever-advancing civilization.

In most aspects of life the ability to be flexible and adaptable is a strength which brings about healthy adjustment to change. However, in the case of our spiritual obligations, it is necessary to be immovable as the mountain, as steady and unchanging as the rock. The spiritual requirements which Bahá'u'lláh has placed upon us in this day are not subject to change, no matter how difficult our circumstances may be. It is at such times that we most need to realign ourselves with the spiritual laws of God's creation because this is the Source of our strength and direction. To enable us to become free of limitations, we must – to ever greater degrees – observe our spiritual obligations of praying, reading and studying the Bahá'í Writings, observing the Fast, teaching, giving to the Fund, attending Feast, practising consultation and striving to exemplify the spiritual qualities that justify our use of the name 'Bahá'í'. Each one of these actions benefits us in a specific way and helps us to fulfil the requirements of our Covenant with Bahá'u'lláh. By observing them regularly we acquire knowledge, divine assistance, spiritual energy, enkindlement and a deeper love for our fellow humans. If we allow times of difficulty to impede and distract us from these obligations, we gradually lose strength and become progressively more burdened and limited at the very time when strength is most needed.

Times of difficulty or crisis are when we most need to call ourselves to account, to evaluate how well we are observing these spiritual obligations. We need to identify the thoughts and actions which are limiting our growth and causing obstacles which block the path of progress. We need to set goals which will assist us to think and act differently in future, in order to meet the higher levels of change or challenge which confront us. As we rise to meet these new degrees, we receive the divine power and guidance sufficient to enable us to sustain them and so our continuing growth is assured.

Therefore, husband and wife need to order their family life in such a way that this essential spiritual foundation receives the consideration which it deserves. This requires regular opportunity for consultation, involving both parents and children, so that the needs of each family member are continually being taken into account and planned for. This on-going interest and concern in the lives of each member creates an environment of nurturing, security and love.

The use of goals and plans was the method established by 'Abdu'l-Bahá, and continued by both the Guardian and the Universal House of Justice, to ensure the sustained growth of an international Bahá'í community. At no time have we been left without wise and considered goals to set our direction, or plans to bring them about; and these goals and plans require the commitment of every level from the individual to the world community. The plans in which we participate give us a sense of belonging, interdependence and common purpose. They create reliance and trust in our hearts towards those who are guiding and watching over us. These are also the feelings which wise and careful parenting can foster within families. Families must consult to establish direction and requirements. They must encourage the development of goals for both individual and collective life, so that each member feels supported and sustained and has a clear personal plan for growth. In this way the family becomes progressively freed of limitations in thought and action.

Consideration will be given in this and in following chapters to practical means of encouraging a smooth transition and progress through the passages of life. Approaches will include planning for flexibility in organization and occupation, identifying and utilizing resources, implementing consultation, and family decision-making, planning and goal-setting.

Strengthening the Marriage Relationship

If the relationship of supreme priority in our lives is with our Creator, the second priority is with our marriage partner. It is a popular theory of human relationships that satisfaction of our personal needs must take precedence over others for the reason that if the individual's primary needs – first for survival and health and then for security, stability, social interaction, self-esteem and self-actualization – are not satisfied on a basic level first, then one lacks a foundation upon which to give support to others.

This identification of priorities is often called a hierarchy of needs. Having a clear and agreed idea of the relative importance of things is very useful when there are many matters requiring the attention of an individual or a group. The ability to assess quickly which matters require priority is valuable in marriages and families because it ensures that members are operating according to one defined value system which has the support of all. Today, when the pace of life exerts such pressure and when every Bahá'í feels a sense of urgency because there seems so much to do and so little time in which to do it, the ability to know what to do first is precious. If the marriage partners cannot agree on what takes priority, the stage is easily set for conflict. On the other hand, if values are agreed upon in advance then, when problems arise, the partners can work from an established base of unity and agreement, if necessary modifying the system as experience and circumstances dictate.

The new age in which we live brings with it new perspectives, values and priorities to replace outdated forms. An old hierarchy of needs showing the place of marriage and family may have identified the priorities as follows:

GOD — HUSBAND — LIVESTOCK — MALE CHILDREN — WIFE — FEMALE CHILDREN

This reflects both the traditional superiority of man over woman and the high value placed upon some means of livelihood which would ensure the survival of the group. A hierarchy reflecting the values of the present, often irreligious and self-serving age might identify priorities as follows:

SELF — CAREER — PARTNER — POSSESSIONS — CHILDREN

A Bahá'í hierarchy of needs naturally places one's relationship with God as the first priority. In marriage and family life we are responsible, not only for our own relationships to God, but also to a degree for those of our partners and children. Husband and wife must 'ever improve the spiritual life of each other'[3] and must educate their children to know and worship God.

Where, then, is the place of self? Many hierarchies place self first and include one's spiritual needs amongst many others such as self-actualization and self-esteem. Unfortunately, this is often used to justify preferring oneself over others, when the Bahá'í injunction is to prefer others before oneself, even to become forgetful of self. It also overlooks the reality that 'no man is an island'. 'Abdu'l-Bahá explained:

> It seems as though all creatures can exist singly and alone. For example, a tree can exist solitary and alone on a given prairie or in a valley or on the mountainside. An animal upon a mountain or a bird soaring in the air might live a solitary life. They are not in need of cooperation or solidarity. Such animated beings enjoy the greatest comfort and happiness in their respective solitary lives.
>
> On the contrary, man cannot live singly and alone. He is in need of continuous cooperation and mutual help. For example, a man living alone in the wilderness will eventually starve. He can never, singly and alone, provide himself with all the necessities of existence. Therefore, he is in need of cooperation and reciprocity . . .
>
> Although the body politic is one family yet because of lack of harmonious relations some members are comfortable and some in direst misery, some members are satisfied and some are hungry, some members are clothed in most costly garments and some families are in need of food and shelter. Why? Because this family lacks the necessary reciprocity and symmetry. This household is not well arranged. This household is not living under a perfect law. All the laws which are legislated do not ensure happiness. They do not provide comfort. Therefore a law must be given to this family by means of which all the members of this family

will enjoy equal well-being and happiness.

Is it possible for one member of a family to be subjected to the utmost misery and to abject poverty and for the rest of the family to be comfortable? It is impossible unless those members of the family be senseless, atrophied, inhospitable, unkind . . .

Such utter indifference in the human family is due to lack of control, to lack of a working law, to lack of kindness in its midst. If kindness had been shown to the members of this family surely all the members thereof would have enjoyed comfort and happiness.[4]

The reality is that none of us can live in isolation, that the ideal is to work together to satisfy the needs of one another and to use to fullest advantage the power that exists in working together in unity. The observations made by 'Abdu'l-Bahá in respect of the macrocosm, the family of humanity, are equally true of the microcosm, the individual family unit; for as has been discussed, it is here that we first exercise the principles that foster cooperation and solidarity and implement them practically.

The atmosphere in a Bahá'í home is one of reciprocity, of mutual support where no one prefers himself or herself before others. It is a 'no lose' environment. Because the real needs of all are valued and freely satisfied no one can 'win' at the expense of another. Such disregard for the well-being of our wider family of humanity has been the cause of appalling inequity and suffering. If 'Abdu'l-Bahá has judged humanity to be senseless, atrophied, inhospitable and unkind in this broader sense, how much more blameworthy would He consider such disregard for the well-being of the members of our own family units?

A previous section described ignorance as being one of the greatest limitations to the progress of humans. Selfishness is another. The progress of one individual at the expense of another is pure illusion, for ultimately the price for such inequity must be paid, even as we are now paying a price for exploiting our fellow humans and our environment. It is also a mark of limited thinking to assume that if one person is to benefit, then another must go without.

Here is an example of such limiting thought. A subject is brought forward for consultation. On the face of it, members have needs which do not readily complement each other. It is all too easy to approach the solution with an either/or expectation – one person will have his or her needs satisfied and the other must accept his or her differing needs as incompatible and impossible to satisfy. Such limited thinking is still a prime cause of global conflict – many people claim world peace is impossible because no forum could be capable of reconciling the diverse needs of humankind. How can Bahá'ís hope to achieve world peace when in our own families we place our personal needs before those of others and consider it reasonable that only one set of needs can be fulfilled? In this day the power of unity is sufficient to reconcile such situations to the benefit of all, if the principles of consultation are respected. Indeed, it is in the home that we must perfect the tools of unity which we would have others accept and practise.

What is needed is a concept of priority or hierarchy which allows us to have consideration for the well-being of all but also acknowledges that within that broader context we must identify narrower and more specific goals which only we can fulfil. We must do the most important things first. The well-being of humanity depends upon the well-being of nations and then of the families of which it is comprised. Families in turn are dependent upon the quality of parenting, which again is a reflection of the individual's relationship to God.

Therefore, a Bahá'í hierarchy of needs might be expressed as:

GOD – MARRIAGE – CHILDREN – SERVICE TO MANKIND

Such a clear identification of priorities is helpful in reconciling many of the apparent incompatibilities which exist at times within Bahá'í families. There are many occasions when the changes and circumstances of life oblige partners to find solutions from a seemingly narrow and less than ideal range of options. Some examples of situations which, if met to the satisfaction of only one person, could place considerable constraints on others, are as follows:

- the need to relocate the home in order to satisfy the requirements of the breadwinner's occupation

- the necessity for one partner to be away from home for significant periods to meet the needs of occupation or Bahá'í service

- the need to entertain business clients at home

- the ability to respond to an occupation's long, inflexible, unsocial or unpredictable work hours

- the desire of one partner either to increase or to limit the number of offspring.

One area of Bahá'í life requiring thoughtful consideration on the part of marriage partners is how best to serve the needs of the Faith and also the needs of the family. The model of a possible Bahá'í hierarchy of priorities identifies no specific category for Bahá'í service. Instead, it acknowledges the need for us to apply Bahá'í principles and practices to every sphere of our lives. It represents an holistic approach to Bahá'í service which allows us to give our greatest attention to whatever is the greatest need, and this is continually varying according to circumstance.

To give a specific example, a Bahá'í mother naturally wishes to be of service to her community, to teach, to attend events, to support the administration. An opportunity arises to serve on a committee in an area in which she has unique expertise. However, the family also wants more of her time and, in particular, her husband feels that, in the flurry of everyday life, they are losing touch with one another. The first point to acknowledge is that this does not have to be an either/or situation, where a simple choice must be made between Bahá'í service on the one hand and marriage and family on the other. The second point to recognize is that where there are many important things to do, the partners may have agreed that the needs of family take priority over service to mankind. Other Bahá'ís may serve on the committee, even if they do not possess the same experience, but no one else can be the wife and mother of that family. There are many possible outcomes which consultation may produce. The husband may consider that a special night together away from the family every two weeks would be sufficient to sustain the warmth and intimacy of the relationship. The family may agree to have a special 'family only' day once every month devoted to pleasurable activities. The committee might be able to draw upon the mother's skills in a purely advisory capacity and consequently benefit from her expertise without requiring her to attend all its meetings. Through consultation, a way can be found in which all needs could be met and each aspect given the priority which it deserves.

In another example, the husband is the primary breadwinner and the wife has worked for many years in an unpaid position of responsibility for a community service organization. Their children have grown up and live away from home. In order for the husband to remain at his present level within the company he must move to a branch in another, much smaller town. However, the wife would have to give up the employment which she loves and she would be unlikely to find a similar occupation in the new town as it is so small.

The first priority which the partners identify here is the family, as the husband's occupation is their only means of livelihood. An important secondary value is service to humanity. Both partners value their occupations because they each provide an opportunity for service which benefits their community, and each partner performs his or her work in the spirit of service, making the work an act of worship. This is an important point: the husband's career is valued because it contributes to the well-being of the family and not because career, or income-earning, is an end in itself. And even though only one partner is earning a livelihood, the work of both is valued as constituting a form of worship and service to humanity. This family may decide that, as there are no longer any dependents to support, they can afford to take a cut in income so that both can continue at occupations which serve a valuable function. Another choice is to make the move to the new area where, due to small numbers, their contributions to the teaching work of the Faith would be even more valuable. The wife might take correspondence courses which would enable her to gain a significant qualification in the area in which she has worked in a voluntary and limited way in the past.

In a different situation, the husband is the chief breadwinner. The wife is pregnant and works at managing the household and running a small freelance business from home. The husband's job as a salesperson is extremely demanding, sometimes requiring him to be away for a week or more, or to work erratic, unpredictable hours. His income is good but his wife misses his company and feels very isolated and lacking in stimulation. In addition, she is often unwell and has no one apart from her husband to care for her. However, in the husband's job there is no provision to take time off to care for an ill family member and his employer is already unhappy when he and his wife telephone one another during work hours or when he leaves the office in his lunch hour to spend time caring for her. The major factors in this situation are the needs of the marriage and the family, including the unborn child. The husband is responsible for the family's security and for providing a livelihood which will ensure the well-being of the family. However, in this case it seems the reverse is fast becoming true: the happiness of wife, child and consequently the husband are adversely affected by the inflexibility of his occupation. The marriage partners may decide that in spite of any resulting economic hardship, it is more important to ensure the security and support of wife and child through a change in occupation to a less well-paid but more flexible job. They may decide that both will work from home in a freelance capacity so that the husband is in a better situation to care for them. Alternatively, he could remain in his job which provides good material security and use the extra income to pay for competent household assistance and nursing care if necessary, freeing himself of all other obligations so that his non-working hours are exclusively for the benefit of his family.

A following section will consider in greater detail another situation which is increasingly common to Bahá'í families: how best to reconcile the apparently contradictory roles which may be filled by a Bahá'í woman – receiving an education, entering into typically male spheres of influence, breadwinning, household management, and the bearing and education of children.

Strengthening the Family

'Abdu'l-Bahá, in one of the quotations cited above,

indicated some of the qualities and conditions which exist in the ideal household. These qualities fall into broad groups. The first qualities are those that constitute a state of unity – cooperation, solidarity, mutual help, reciprocity, sensitivity, kindness and harmonious relations. It is clear that when such a state of unity exists within marriages, family units and the whole human family there is no longer any need for individuals or groups to struggle for their rights. In place of conflict there is harmony. In such a household, women and girls do not have to struggle for equality of opportunity and education and neither do the males feel attacked and resentful. When difficulties and hardship are experienced, those who may be ill, disabled, handicapped, poor or elderly do not feel that they are a burden. When the changes and chances of the world affect any of the members, when the conditions within or without the home are subject to revolution and fluctuation, a sense of security, support and loyalty will enable the family members to rise to the challenge of the moment and transmute difficulty into success.

The forms which the families of the future may take are unknown. Beyond the laws of the *Kitáb-i-Aqdas*, there are no hard and fast rules which govern all families. Even the Universal House of Justice seldom gives definitive injunctions in areas of marriage or family life. The primary consideration is the spirit that has to permeate our collective social life and this will be expressed in principles and structures that will gradually promote ideal conditions. Applying general Bahá'í principles to actual conditions prevailing at any one time, we will eventually bring about profound change – in the relative prosperity of society, in the workplace, in social services, in opportunities for education of the individual and in systems designed to support the family. Such changes, involving specific and detailed solutions to questions facing us even now, will unfold progressively as humankind develops a social system which embodies the spirit and the exact provisions of the Cause. This necessitates a more thorough study of the Bahá'í teachings in the light of modern problems so that we may promote what the Founders of the Faith said and not what we imagine. There is a great difference between expressing a general principle and actually bringing about the fundamental changes which must remodel the complicated relationships of society, preserve the well-being of the family, control the forces which now threaten to disrupt its existence and, in this manner, assert the mastery of human beings over the material world.

Shoghi Effendi has given us a glimpse of wonderful potentialities which will bring about profound changes in the family as we now know it and will enable it to achieve a condition of spiritual and material well-being unimaginable today.

> The economic resources of the world will be organized, its sources of raw materials will be tapped and fully utilized, its markets will be coordinated and developed, and the distribution of its products will be equitably regulated.
>
> . . . The enormous energy dissipated and wasted on war, whether economic or political, will be consecrated to such ends as will extend the range of human inventions and technical development, to the increase of the productivity of mankind, to the extermination of disease, to the extension of scientific research, to the raising of the standard of physical health, to the sharpening and refinement of the human brain, to the exploitation of the unused and unsuspected resources of the planet, to the prolongation of human life, and to the furtherance of any other agency that can stimulate the intellectual, the moral, and spiritual life of the entire human race.
>
> A world federal system, ruling the whole earth and exercising unchallengeable authority over its unimaginably vast resources, blending and embodying the ideals of both

the East and the West, liberated from the curse of war and its miseries, and bent on the exploitation of all the available sources of energy on the surface of the planet, a system in which Force is made the servant of Justice, whose life is sustained by its universal recognition of one God and by its allegiance to one common Revelation – such is the goal towards which humanity, impelled by the unifying forces of life, is moving.[5]

How New Concepts of Work Will Affect the Family

One of the above quotations from the Universal House of Justice established that mothers are not obliged to work for the purpose of gaining a livelihood, that Bahá'u'lláh's directive means that the friends must be engaged in an occupation which will be of benefit to humankind. When we talk about work being identical to worship of God, we often make the assumption that this refers to a breadwinning function. However, even men need only be breadwinners to the extent necessary to satisfy the expenditure requirements of the family, which would include giving to the Fund and contributing to humanitarian purposes. Breadwinning of itself does not necessarily satisfy the aim of being of benefit to humankind: in fact, there are all too many, often well-paid, occupations that are detrimental to the well-being of society.

Again, the important quality for Bahá'ís is that our work is done in the spirit of worship and is of benefit to humanity. This makes no distinction between breadwinning and other types of work, for both are of value and fulfil the same essential function. Viewed in this light, it is impossible to hold the opinion that one's own field of work is in itself of greater account than another's. Thus, it cannot be assumed that a breadwinning role is of more value than mothering, or that the work of a scientist is greater than that of someone who has lovingly fashioned a simple sheet of notepaper to the best of his or her ability. Rather, the values of each can be viewed as relative; in certain circumstances the role of the mother may be of most significance and therefore most in need of support and resources, yet in another case the role of breadwinning, whether by wife or husband, takes priority.

Viewed in the context of service to humanity, it is also not possible to assume that service directly within the Bahá'í community has any greater or lesser value than other areas of beneficial work or service. All should be valued, as all are of potential benefit. However, once again the relative value of each can only be considered in the context of a specific situation. Service to the Bahá'í community should not take precedence over the needs of the marriage or family which is, after all, just a small unit of a larger Bahá'í community. The disunity which might arise from such an action would entirely negate any possible benefit. Indeed, one of the present challenges of the Bahá'í community is to sustain and preserve Bahá'í marriage and family life. How pointless if the progress of community life was counter-productive to the progress of marriage and the family. Rather, the ideal is to achieve a balance, where things are arranged in such a way that both requirements are met and where the work of each member of the family is supported and valued by all. Shoghi Effendi wrote:

> With reference to Bahá'u'lláh's command concerning the engagement of the believers in some sort of profession; the Teachings are most emphatic on this matter, particularly the statement in the 'Aqdas' to this effect which makes it quite clear that idle people who lack the desire to work can have no place in the new World Order. As a corollary of this principle, Bahá'u'lláh further states that mendicity should not only be discouraged but entirely wiped out from

the face of society. It is the duty of those who are in charge of the organization of society to give every individual the opportunity of acquiring the necessary talent in some kind of a profession, and also the means of utilizing such a talent, both for its own sake and for the sake of earning the means of his livelihood. Every individual, no matter how handicapped and limited he may be, is under the obligation of engaging in some work or profession, for work, specially when performed in the spirit of service, is according to Bahá'u'lláh a form of worship. It has not only a utilitarian purpose, but has a value in itself, because it draws us nearer to God, and enables us to better grasp His purpose for us in this world. It is obvious, therefore, that the inheritance of wealth cannot make anyone immune from daily work.[6]

Another ramification of the principle found in the Bahá'í teachings that work is worship is that nowhere is the application of this principle restricted to adults. Such is the direct association between work and breadwinning in the world at large that the contribution of children and youth to service in the home and the community is often not fully encouraged in the sense of fulfilling a spiritual obligation. Of course, it is not intended that children and youth consequently be breadwinners, although unfortunately in all too many cultures this is one of the tragic necessities of survival. 'Abdu'l-Bahá has stated that children should be brought up to work and strive. Unfortunately, for many parents the harsh reality of working life has been such a negative experience that they try to shield children from such unpleasantness until maturity makes it essential. One of the challenges facing us, therefore, is to evolve a thoroughly new concept of the nature of work, to find ways to embue work with the spirit of service and worship. This may come about as we cease to relate it so directly to the obligation to earn a living and free ourselves from the associations of competition, prestige, class and social position which correlate the type of work directly with the worth of the individual.

Other resources which are lamentably untapped, to the detriment of many, are the contributions of the elderly, handicapped, disabled and infirm.

> Even though you are 79 years old, that does not seem in your case to be any handicap; and in this Cause, as the Guardian has told us there is work for everyone of some sort, of whatever age he or she may be.[7]

These members of our society are also subject to the principle that work is worship and is enjoined upon all. It is not kindness or sensitivity to deny any human being the opportunity to serve both the Lord and humankind through some form of work in which he or she may find true value and meaning in life and enjoy the growth and challenges which the rest of society derive from the advantage of useful service. All too often, what is intended to be an alleviation of burden and responsibility on the part of well-meaning individuals is the very means by which a vital sense of purpose, progress and hope is lost. At the same time, families and societies are denied yet another resource and valuable contribution to the common good. The challenge is to educate and train each person to the necessary extent, and to identify and provide useful and stimulating occupations which will utilize individual talents and ability.

Work Options for Mothers

How does consideration of the true value and purpose of a person's occupation assist in formulating new models to satisfy the needs of individual families? An example of the need to find new models is in solving the dilemma facing many mothers today: on the one hand, 'Abdu'l-Bahá has said that women must receive the same education and opportunities as men, must enter fully and capably into fields such as law, the sciences and agriculture and may be breadwinners; on the other hand, women are encouraged to marry, and they are to be the first and primary educators of children. This would seem on the surface to involve super-human, if not totally incompatible, expectations. In their desire to meet such expectations, Bahá'í women may fall prey to rising levels of ill-health, increasingly associated with stress. Husbands may become frustrated by their inability to understand and meet the increased demands and expectations placed upon them by wives. Children may find their parents are becoming progressively more remote, strained and pressured at the very time when those children are feeling overwhelmed by the effects of unparalleled and frightening change. Knowledge of what the Writings require enables one, first, to identify boundaries and restrictions within which one must work and, consequently, to recognize broad areas of freedom and choice which exist within those limits. Some considerations which may help clarify and define solutions are as follows:

- Mothering takes priority. The family needs to identify the extent of 'hands on' mothering required, i.e. the aspects of direct childcare which can only, or ideally, be performed by the mother. Obviously, older children and youth require increasingly less attention. Some children may actually be more in need of the qualities of a father.

  In past ages, mothers have always undertaken roles in addition to their child-rearing functions. Many of these roles have been bound up in satisfying the basic needs of survival. In this century, establishing the means of survival is still a main feature of life for women in many parts of the world; this is largely assured for Western families. All women face the challenge of how best to use their God-given abilities in satisfying ways, but the loneliness, isolation and lack of stimulation experienced by housebound mothers of nuclear Western families who are shut away in dormitory suburbs from the city centres of activity, influence and decision-making is a relatively recent phenomenon.

• What is desired in the nature of education, occupation or profession? Mothering and home management are praiseworthy occupations. However, the requirements of these occupations fluctuate. All children grow up and for those parents whose work is home management, there should still be time for other, diversified, services and occupations.

There may be sufficient time apart from any roles within the home to take advantage of continuing education. Many tertiary education institutions provide quality childcare and courses at hours which can be selected to suit family circumstances. They also offer adjustable course requirements which can better meet the often unpredictable conditions experienced by students who are also mothers. Part-time study may, over the years, accrue into significant qualifications, offering more choice in later life and allowing the individual to develop more fully her God-given capacities so as to provide a stimulating balance with duties centred on the home. The ability to earn a living from one's skills is a valuable asset and offers the family greater choices; when both partners are capable of breadwinning there may be times when it is an advantage for the husband to work only part-time or not at all. The partners may wish to reverse roles so that the husband can give his attention to other occupations, perhaps child-rearing or charitable or educational enterprises, or so that the mother may newly enjoy the challenges and rewards of full-time occupation while he attends to tasks previously filled by her. The ability of more than one family member to earn an income also allows them to adjust more easily to the illness, disability, unemployment or death of the primary income-earner. In addition, a family member may require attendant care due to illness or age; flexibility in breadwinning creates more options for family members to meet this need.

Freelance work from home with hours adjusted to suit may be possible for a woman in the home, allowing her to build up her clientèle as time allows, perhaps eventually to become full-time. The flexible hours create opportunities for many types of charitable work which may be undertaken as a service to humanity on behalf of the family as a whole. Similarly, the family may deputize the mother to be their 'teacher' – to travel teach, deepen at institutes, host firesides which the rest of the family may support by helping with hospitality. She may also be considered as the family's representative in Bahá'í community service, dedicating her life to fulfilling the many and diverse functions which are a necessary part of the administrative, teaching and service aspects of a community. This is worthy of the active support of the entire family and by no means a 'poor relation' to the work of the breadwinner; a person fulfilling such a role is entitled to equal means of support both emotionally and physically. Of course, this could equally apply to fathers when a mother becomes the breadwinner.

The period of time in which occupations must be combined with mothering can provide valuable opportunities to train for a new occupation or to seek out an occupation which is similar to a previous one but has better conditions – such as more flexible hours, better child-care provisions and greater opportunities to expand into new and challenging areas. There may be opportunities to change direction into an area which is either compatible with, or an extension of, the previous one. Alternatively, a complete break in previous occupation may be the very means of being guided into a situation, or innovatively creating one, which makes even better use of skills, talents and abilities. Of course, the family may just resolve to throw in their present situation and head off pioneering!

- The family needs to identify other human resources which can be used to the benefit of both dependent child and mother. Apart from obvious helpers such as husband, grandparents, aunts, uncles, etc., the assistance of other children and youth within the family should be utilized. These important family members have the privilege and obligation to be of service and yet so often reach adulthood unprepared to shoulder the responsibilities of homes and families. In many countries even children as young as four years are given roles in relation to their baby brothers and sisters, which they discharge with care and dependability, thereby learning valuable lessons in family life and future childcare.

In addition to the option of paid, professional childcare either in the home or at childcare centres, it may be found that a pleasurable, reciprocal relationship may be established with others who enjoy being an 'adopted' and contributing family member, with its attendant privileges and rewards. A previous chapter described how the Holy Household was a place of refuge, solace and satisfaction to many 'adopted' members who, like any true family member, both gave and received. Studies indicate that in childcare which is supplemental to the role of the mother, crucial factors for success are continuity, consistency, security and quality of human relationship. Over the ages, many cultures have taken advantage of multiple carers to provide for the needs of the community's young children. Common elements among the carers are that they share the same essential value system, that they support and reinforce one another and that they are strong in qualities of loving and nurturing.

Bahá'í families should consider drawing on the love, strength and assistance of other Bahá'í families in their areas. In a letter written on his behalf the Guardian said:

> . . . the believers have not yet fully learned to draw on each other's love for strength and consolation in time of need.[8]

It may be that mothers with children of a similar age can share childcare from time to time, freeing each mother occasionally for other work or service. It may be possible for them, with their children, to form a 'teaching group' and together share the joys of teaching new people about the Faith. Those of us who are perhaps free of certain administrative obligations might consider offering to look after the home and children of a family where the mother or both parents are elected to Local or National Spiritual Assemblies or are appointed as Auxiliary Board Members or Assistants. This may be considered a subject worthy of consultation at a Nineteen Day Feast or Assembly meeting and may be considered as a 'social development' project.

The solutions that may be found to enable women to carry out their multiple and changing roles will differ from family to family, according to circumstances. Solutions will also reflect the range of options provided by communities which must increasingly come to acknowledge, and give priority to, the need for special provisions to enable women to achieve equality of opportunity in education, family life and workplace.

6

Family Consultation as a Tool for Progress

The Happy Family is a children's story-book. On its rosy-coloured pages mum is forever cooking the roast dinner, dad is going off to work and returning to mow the lawn while son helps dad and daughter picks the flowers. While many of us would not consider this a picture of a real family, it may be that there are good reasons for the roles each member of this family plays: this may be poor old sedentary dad's only opportunity in his whole desk-bound week for a spot of exercise and mum may enjoy gourmet cookery. What is amusing is that they do this all so effortlessly. What happens, one could ask, when mum's gourmet cookery class conflicts with dad's office party? What will happen if dad's health forces him to leave the job or he finds himself unemployed for other reasons, or if mum tires of cookery and wants to go full-time to the local technical institute to learn a trade? It's a bit like looking at the face of a beautiful clock but not knowing what makes it tick. How do we make our families work? Many of us have grown up expecting that, like *The Happy Family*, everything will just somehow fall effortlessly into place. Suddenly things start happening that weren't in the 'script' and we feel helpless, as if we're trapped in a game for which we haven't been taught the rules.

The Organic Nature of the Bahá'í Family

Change can be very frightening if we haven't learned to use it as a catalyst for growth, as a new and exciting opportunity. The past may seem far more desirable than the present or future, for it is a known quantity – it holds no surprises, asks nothing new. Consequently many people are returning, in both political and religious matters, to past philosophies, to conservatism and fundamentalism, with some becoming almost fanatically opposed to change or innovation because it seems so threatening. However, doing this is to neglect one basic rule of thumb which can be applied to all aspects of life: if something isn't growing and changing then it's probably dead.

The previous chapter established the fact that Bahá'ís see change as both essential and desirable; change is the indicator of life and progress. In the words of 'Abdu'l-Bahá:

> Know that nothing which exists remains in a state of repose – that is to say, all things are in motion. Everything is either growing or declining . . .[1]

It is impossible for us to avoid change; all we can do is to choose whether we will grow or decline, which isn't such a difficult choice!

However we organize our families we must make provision for this factor of change; and not just allow it but encourage it in positive and progressive ways. This approach is what is often termed an 'open' system as opposed to a 'closed' system. A 'closed' system exists when the individuals strive – and are destined to fail – to maintain a given set of circumstances, to avoid change. One of the theories of the 'closed' system is that the individuals who control it can make up a list of rules and procedures to apply for all time and then simply ensure that these are enforced. An extensive set of threats and punishments is generally required in order to maintain control because those who are being controlled are unable to make any personal input in decision-making and are denied the rewards of self-achievement. This creates dissatisfaction and frustration. In the traditional authoritarian family, the father is the controller and the mother and children are subordinate. Such a 'closed' system family is like an office block built to a precise specification: the structure is firm, perhaps even strong, but lifeless.

By contrast, the Bahá'í family is organic; it is a living and growing thing like a plant, bringing forth flowers and fruits. One cannot 'plant' a family and then conveniently walk away from it; it requires continual watering, feeding and, occasionally, pruning. In other words, because the Bahá'í family is always changing, its members must frequently pause to consider its stage of growth and to assess its needs. They must foster further growth by careful planning and provision, by praise, love and encouragement and by judicious preventative or punitive measures if a decline takes place or if growth becomes imbalanced. It is this recognition of the *organic* nature of humankind that is so much in contrast with historic attitudes towards the family and upon which we need to focus continually if we are not to fall back upon mere imitation of the past. We must recognize that our single family group represents one twig upon the great and all-embracing tree of humankind, that the welfare of all is in part dependent upon our own individual welfare and vice versa. As we apply the principles of the Faith to our own families – as we practise consultation, freedom from prejudice, the equality of men and women, the education of children, hospitality, teaching the Faith and other facets of family life – so we introduce these principles into the great body of humankind. This is the true teaching of the Faith – that we let deeds, not words, be our adorning.

A Source of Guidance and Understanding

The process that facilitates organic development is consultation: it is the method whereby the gardeners of the human world ascertain the needs of their plants and provide for optimum growth.

Bahá'u'lláh says:

> Take ye counsel together in all matters, inasmuch as consultation is the lamp of guidance which leadeth the way, and is the bestower of understanding.[2]

This is the process that is used at every level of the great human family, be it the single family unit, Local Spiritual Assembly, National Spiritual Assembly or Universal House of Justice; for how could a procedure that is beneficial to one branch not also be beneficial to the whole tree? It is an on-going process. The plant that needs feeding today may not need feeding again next week but its new growth may need staking; if unbalanced it may need pruning. Similarly, our family structures must make provision for on-going consultation, whether formally, by setting aside a particular time each week for family consultation, for example, or informally, as opportunity or the need arises. One difficulty in this latter approach is that the family may only consult once a problem arises, by which stage feelings of disunity and dissatisfaction may be well-established and hard to deal with. This is not to say that any family can avoid problems from arising at all; problems and tests are one of the ways in which we grow and learn. However, some may be anticipated by thoughtful forward planning and others may be completely avoided or used in very positive ways.

An example of this last method is the gardener who has a big binge in the garden once and then leaves it alone until weeds begin choking the flowers and a few plants have been blown over by storms. She is gardening as the need arises. Her neighbour, on the other hand, wanders through her garden every few days for the sheer pleasure of watching things grow; she pulls each weed while it is small and easily removed and, seeing dark clouds on the horizon, stakes her plants in preparation. She is well informed of the requirements of plants both from personal experience and from other sources open to her and knows the importance of planning ahead for crop rotation and the like. Although she and her neighbour began their gardens at the same time, hers bears many more fruits and flowers for the benefit of others.

The gardener of the vegetable world must rely upon observation and research alone to understand the needs of her plants; the gardener of the human world also possesses the ability to consult with her charges. It is the duty of the parents to ensure that they are continually aware of the needs of those for whom they are responsible. Just as in prayer we are able to commune with God and state our needs with the assurance that our prayers will be heard and answered, so we parents should make ourselves available to our family members. We need to become aware of our own needs and to be able to state these as clearly as possible and to encourage our children to do the same. We should share our hopes and plans with them when applicable and help them to understand why we do things in certain ways – for example, why a particular action of the child's required discipline, what standards we expect of each other and why these standards are important.

Children and Consultation

Increasingly over the last few decades the expressions 'communication breakdown' or 'generation gap' have been used to describe symptoms of the collapse of society at large and the family in particular. Perhaps we can recall

our own despair as children in trying to cope with
problems which seemed of earth-shaking proportions and
feeling that our parents were totally unsympathetic to our
needs. Maybe, back in those 'olden days', what passed for
consultation seemed to go something like this: 'Please
Dad, can I . . .?' 'No, you can't.' 'O gee, why not?'
'Because I said so.' 'But that's not fair!' 'Don't answer
back!' We hated this if this happened to us, and our
children will like it even less, especially if at other times we
encourage them to look into all things with a seeing eye,
urge them to investigate truth independently, and extol
the virtues of free and frank consultation.

As Bahá'ís, our first attempts at consultation on an
Assembly are, for most of us, pretty nerve-racking. It's
hard not to interrupt when you feel quite sure that what
you're about to say will be of profound significance to
everyone else, particularly when so-and-so has been so
obstinate and pig-headed – and if everyone insists on
having his two cents' worth, no one will get home until
midnight.

Our children, however, will not have to face these
difficulties. As soon as their vocabulary first grows wide
enough for them to express themselves, they will learn
that in all things it is necessary to consult. They will use
consultation to agree on standards of bedroom tidiness, on
household chores, on which movies to see with their
brother or sister. Their thoughts and opinions will be
called upon when Mum and Dad are deciding where to go
on the family holiday or when to pioneer or just what time
to set for each child's bedtime. They will be aware of the
principles of the Faith which apply to consultation and will
be able to apply those principles in their own lives quite
naturally. The families of such children will have put into
practice this guidance of the Universal House of Justice:

Bahá'u'lláh came to bring unity to the world, and a

fundamental unity is that of the family. Therefore, one must believe that the Faith is intended to strengthen the family, not weaken it, and one of the keys to the strengthening of unity is loving consultation. The atmosphere within a Bahá'í family as within the community as a whole should express 'the keynote of the Cause of God' which, the beloved Guardian has stated, 'is not dictatorial authority but humble fellowship, not arbitrary power, but the spirit of frank and loving consultation'.[3]

Not dictatorial authority but humble fellowship – what an extraordinary attitude for us to express to one another, let alone to our children. At a time when it is popular to describe the ways in which people relate to one another in terms of 'power' and 'assertiveness', qualities of love, humility and fellowship stand in marked contrast. It is one thing to apply the spirit of humble fellowship to our fellow members in the community who, after all, may be older or wiser or wealthier or more educated than ourselves; however, to apply it to the parent-to-child relationship – where the parent is responsible for the training of the child and the child is expected to be obedient and respectful towards the parent – requires some consideration.

A popular T-shirt reads 'Children are people too'. The sentiment this expresses is so very true. The term 'child', whilst it can be used in a symbolic sense to denote someone who is a novice in a particular area, generally refers to a person under the age of majority who is still under the responsibility of his parents. In no way does the term indicate that that child is less worthy than his parents or others. In fact, in Bahá'í history there are many stories of children who were far superior to adults in their degree of spirituality. Unlike those adult believers who may not recognize Bahá'u'lláh until many decades of ignorance and wrong living have taken their toll, these children of Bahá have the opportunity to grow and develop from the beginning in an atmosphere of spirituality and divine bounty. We adults can learn so much from these children, if we can only avoid the patronizing attitude which is too easily substituted for true humble fellowship. The principle of equality applies to adults and children too. In the book *The Prophet*, Kahlil Gibran describes the parent's relationship to the child:

> Your children are not your children.
> They are the sons and daughters of Life's
>   longing for itself.
> They come through you but not from you.
> And though they are with you yet they belong
>   not to you.[4]

Perhaps on reading these lines we recall childhoods past and the inner knowledge that we were not our parents' possessions but worthy people deserving of respect in our own right.

Within many a rebellious and destructive child is a frustrated person who has very definite and valuable ideas about his or her life, loved ones and environment but who is allowed no expression of those ideas, is denied any personal contribution to the family he or she adores, and whose only function is to be there and carry out the directives from above. Yet Bahá'u'lláh tells us that man – including, of course, women and children – is 'a mine rich in gems of inestimable value' and that education alone can 'cause it to reveal its treasures, and enable mankind to benefit therefrom'.[5] What magnificent contributions can be expected in the future of Bahá'í babies who may have been the subject of more prayers prior to birth than many of us experience in our whole lives!

The parent–child relationship requires balance: an attitude of fellowship towards our children does not preclude discipline. There is a time for everything and a need for moderation. Although children should be able to express themselves, this should take place at suitable times and in the manner of true consultation; it is not a licence for children to have everyone's undivided attention whenever they feel like making a pronouncement on any matter. A child can be likened to a beautiful rose bush: the rose needs watering and feeding and protection from harsh conditions but it also needs regular shaping and pruning. A rose that is allowed to run wild will not benefit from this freedom. Rather, the plant will be progressively weakened and bear fewer and fewer blooms until it is fit only for the fire.

According to the Bahá'í teachings, a child is not directly responsible for his or her own spiritual development until maturity at about 15 years of age. Until then, responsibility rests with the parents. Therefore the final decision on any matter of general family consultation usually rests with the parents, although often all members of the family will be in agreement anyway. This is similar to the way in which Spiritual Assemblies may invite the views of non-Assembly members who have a specific interest or knowledge bearing upon the subject under discussion. However, only the Assembly members themselves have a direct say in decision-making and that decision then becomes binding on the Bahá'í community at large. Even in this case, however, if the decision later appears inadequate or becomes outdated or irrelevant, the subject will be re-introduced for consultation because the factors of change and growth are ever present.

Family Decision-Making

Having described the need for consultation in order to understand and provide for the requirements of the family, consideration must be given to applying the decisions and guidance which derive from it. Much conflict is experienced within families when one member refuses to abide by a decision or simply forgets to apply it. Sometimes the decision or rule or policy hasn't been formulated in sufficient detail to give adequate guidance or it may fail adequately to take into account the needs of all affected. Many of the symptoms of marriage break-down which partners describe to counsellors reflect these problems: disharmony due to misunderstanding of suppos-edly mutual decision-making, or repeated failure of the consultation to provide for the needs of one partner.

When an Assembly creates a particular policy, because human memory is fallible, the policy is recorded carefully for future reference and the details are, when appropriate, conveyed to the community at large. Over a period of time a substantial body of policy is formed which provides specific guidance for an ever-widening range of eventualities. From time to time a policy will require amendment. If the Assembly is in close unity with the community it serves, it can, to a certain extent, anticipate the need for amendment before a crisis makes it all too painfully obvious and disunity arises.

Similarly, when a Bahá'í family formulates a policy, a record of it is often useful. To avoid misunderstanding or forgetfulness, it may be a good idea to record the policy in written form for the information of all. Children will particularly appreciate being able to refer to the policy record as their memories are less developed. Such a record is also an assurance that justice will prevail as no one can change the rules to suit himself and everyone's best interests are served through adherence to the policies.

This 'meeting procedure' approach to consultation may seem unnecessarily ordered and restrictive at first. How-ever, if our businesses rely on this procedure for their successful functioning (can you imagine a business doing without a secretary and the managers simply 'remembering' what was discussed!) then our families, which are even more important to us, should not be afraid of trying more effective and successful methods of planning and decision-making, whatever they may be.

As new situations continually present themselves, the family will, as a matter of course, create new policies and alter or abandon old ones. Like the Assembly with its community, the wise parents will be in such close relationship with all family members that the day-to-day tests and difficulties of ordinary life will never damage the family's fundamental reality but rather serve further to strengthen and develop it.

Planning for Future Progress

The Bahá'í parent must be concerned with both the material and the spiritual needs of the family. 'Abdu'l-Bahá describes two aspects of progress:

> Progress is of two kinds: material and spiritual. The former is attained through observation of the surrounding existence and constitutes the foundation of civilization. Spiritual progress is through the breaths of the Holy Spirit and is the awakening of the conscious soul of man to perceive the reality of Divinity. Material progress ensures the happiness of the human world. Spiritual progress ensures the happiness and eternal continuance of the soul.[6]

The needs of the family can be divided into two areas: those which concern the material progress of the family and ensure happiness in the human world, and those which concern its spiritual progress. By wisely providing for both types of need, the parents can teach the family to tread the spiritual path with practical feet. The Bahá'í Writings give us guidelines for providing for both types of needs and help us to find the balance for those times when treading the path of material and spiritual progress seems more like walking a tightrope. It is easy during those times when we are on a spiritual 'cloud nine' to overlook the fact that our accounts are overdrawn, that the car's warrant of fitness has expired and that the children need new shoes. Then come those times when mere day-to-day existence seems to sap all our energy, the time between prayers gets longer and longer, giving to the Fund is the last item on a long list of expenses and holding a fireside at home seems far less important than that long-awaited opportunity just to put one's feet up in front of a cosy fire and have a nice, quiet evening at home.

Through regular opportunities to consult, the needs of the family can be evaluated and provision made for future progress. Here are a few examples of the two areas within which that progress will take place:

Material

- distribution of household chores
- family budgeting, payment of accounts
- family holidays
- home improvements
- deciding whether to buy a new car or a clothes drier
- deciding which TV programmes the children may watch

Spiritual

- planning for the education of the children
- giving to the Fund
- planning firesides in the home every nineteen days
- fostering family prayer and reading of the Writings
- providing hospitality, hosting Feasts and Holy Days
- teaching the Faith

Even those areas described as 'material' are still subject to spiritual principles. For example, the distribution of chores necessitates setting standards of cleanliness and tidiness, and allocating the workload equitably. Family budgeting should provide for giving to the Fund. Our planning for holidays can take into account attending summer school or travel teaching if we wish. In this sense there is no distinction between material and spiritual progress; any decision made concerning one should also be evaluated in light of the other. This is keeping the balance.

Policy-making and problem-solving are two areas requiring consultation. However, like the wise gardener, families need to plan ahead if they are not merely to subsist from one problem to another. Through consultation both short term and long term goals can be formulated for each individual and for the family as a whole. Long term planning may consider such things as the career or educational goals of members, plans for homefront or overseas pioneering, family and individual teaching goals (e.g. firesides in the home), preparations for pilgrimage, attendance at overseas or local conferences or summer schools and budgeting for major expenses.

Short term planning may express, for example, the need to strengthen a particular spiritual quality (e.g. avoidance of backbiting), or the desire to commence regular dawn prayers. It can also be used to plan the events of the coming week, to list and perform chores around the home or to evaluate earlier plans and policies.

Goal-Setting: Knowledge, Volition and Action

Goal-setting and goal achievement are essential to transform knowledge of principles into real action. 'Abdu'l-Bahá says:

Mere knowledge of principles is not sufficient. We all know

and admit that justice is good but there is need of volition and action to carry out and manifest it.[7]

He also exhorts us to have 'high resolves and noble purposes'.[8] The knowledge that we acquire through studying the Writings morning and night, reading related Bahá'í literature and attending community deepenings should find expression through planning and action. Otherwise of what purpose is this study if we find no practical application for it? Bahá'u'lláh warns us of enterprises which begin in words and end in words. A later chapter will examine ways in which we can compare our present application of Bahá'í principles within our families with the standards expected of the followers of Bahá'u'lláh.

The process of acquiring knowledge and transforming it into action is the process by which we educate ourselves, by which we grow. We live in a society which places most emphasis on the state education provided between the ages of five and sixteen; in other words, it equates 'schooling' with education. Consequently many people leave school considering that their education is at an end.

In most facets of general life, society looks to the period of schooling to supply the basic knowledge. We learn the basic elements of reading, mathematics, natural sciences, cooking, sewing, woodwork, etc. Towards the end of our schooling, the programmes become more and more career-orientated with academic, scientific, technical or commercial courses. After leaving school most children will enter a paid occupation and will become parents. The irony is that most education is directed towards the former and none or very little to the latter. We live in a time when training and qualifications are required in order to be considered responsible enough to operate motor vehicles but none are required to become directly responsible for human lives.

This is one example of the extent to which the Bahá'í teachings are above and beyond current thought and attitude. It emphasizes the need for Bahá'ís to be more than outstanding leaders of present society: we must be innovators. True guidance on Bahá'í family life cannot be found in the 'Family' section of the local library, although some of what can be found there will be in accord with our teachings. We must go to the source – to the Bahá'í Writings and related literature, to institutes, summer schools and deepenings. We must pray and meditate and study, for knowledge is the first condition of change and progress.

> The attainment of any object is conditioned upon knowledge, volition and action. Unless these three conditions are forthcoming there is no execution or accomplishment.[9]

The Value of Goal-Setting

The successive Plans launched by the Universal House of Justice are perfect examples of goal-setting, giving direction, cohesion and momentum to the labours of an internationally diverse community. Goal-setting has many benefits:

- It fosters constant and sustained progress.

- It highlights strengths which can be drawn upon to overcome difficulties and achieve successes.

- It highlights weaknesses. Our awareness of weaknesses shows us where we need to set further goals.

- The completion of goals brings a sense of victory and achievement which encourages us to seek greater attainments.

- The setting of a goal gives a clear sense of direction. It requires us to establish priorities and gives one central focus for our efforts.

- It transforms empty wishes and hopes into real action and achievement.

- It encourages us to take direct responsibility for our own lives and progress, rather than blaming our present condition on some outside factor and resigning ourselves to it.

Sometimes a goal fails because all the factors which relate to it have not been taken into account. It is important to be aware of the factors which foster successful goal-setting:

- We must sincerely want to change, rather than changing only to please someone else or to avoid guilt.

- Goals which are expressed positively are more successful than goals expressed negatively. For example, the goal 'I will speak positively of others and focus on their good qualities' is expressed encouragingly and gives something to strive towards. The goal 'I will not backbite' speaks of a negative quality and focuses on something to be avoided.

- The goal must be achievable and realistic, otherwise it will be doomed to failure and reinforce inadequacy. A goal to increase donations to the Fund by 50% may run aground the following month if the landlord sets a similar goal and increases the rent or if the person setting the goal failed to take into account some outstanding bills.

- Personal qualities are important. We must have adequate knowledge to sustain each goal. If the goal is to pioneer, then the family members can attend a Pioneers' Conference and also study whatever information is available. They can gain more knowledge by consulting with experienced pioneers. Personal qualities of patience, steadfastness and long-suffering under difficulties will influence the achievement of the goal. Praying for increased spiritual qualities will increase the will or volition to attain.

- Putting a goal on paper gives greater reality to the intention to achieve and helps to express it more specifically. It is also a lasting reminder of the commitment.

- Goals need to be specific and answer the questions 'What – Why – Where – When – How'. Goals which are too general often fail to take into account many crucial factors and are difficult to focus upon clearly. We need to ask:
  - What is the goal?
  - What knowledge do I need to achieve this goal?
  - What are the obstacles I will need to overcome?
  - Why do I want to achieve this?
  - What will be the rewards?
  - Where will it take place?
  - How will it take place; what preparation is needed, what will it cost, what resources will be needed?
  - When will it take place and how often? When will it be accomplished?

One of the greatest obstacles to personal change is the force of habit. The greater the period of time spent in following a particular pattern of behaviour, the more time and energy will be required to change that behaviour. For this reason it is important to set positive goals for our children in their earliest years so that the habits they establish will be positive. These positive habits will become the foundation of continuing personal growth.

An Example of the Goal-Setting Process

Let us imagine that, in consultation, the family has made a decision to implement morning and evening prayer. The first consideration will be to define the goal: it needs to be positive, achievable, realistic, specific and measurable.

The long term goal is that every member will pray every morning and night. However, several specific areas need to be considered. Will they pray as a family or as individuals? The decision is that morning prayers will be said as a family whilst evening prayers will be said individually. The youngest child needs assistance and encouragement in his private prayer. The decision is that as Dad has less chance to spend time with the child during the working week, he will read a bedtime story with the child and help with his prayers whilst Mum helps the older children with homework. Morning prayers raise several other issues. Will the family pray before or after dressing, before or after breakfast? Will the prayers be combined with readings from the Writings? How much time should be spent in prayer? The decision is that Mum will wake the older children while Dad dresses the littlest child. When the family is dressed they will gather in the lounge. One of the older children will have the responsibility each week of having ready the prayer books and a compilation of brief Writings. He or she may choose the subject of the Writings. The time spent in prayer will, in general, allow for two prayers per person and a reading.

This seems to be a satisfactory expression of what the family wants as a longer term goal. However, they decide to implement the goal gradually. First they decide to establish morning prayers. At the end of the first week they will come together for another consultation to review their goal and prepare the next stage.

A week passes and the family gathers for consultation. In general, they are very pleased with the result. Family prayers have taken place on each morning of the past week. However, some obstacles have been identified. On two occasions Mum forgot to set the alarm, the family slept in and the prayers needed to be rushed through to make up time. The weekend was a problem as not everyone rose at the same time. The family amends some decisions. Family prayer will now take place every weekday with individual prayer at weekends. Mum will set herself a personal goal to set her alarm every bedtime. At the end of the week, stage two – evening prayers – will be considered.

The second week is a great success. In consultation, plans are made for implementing evening prayer. Several points are raised. The older children think their biggest problem will be in remembering to do the new behaviour every night. Mum suggests that she and the children can draw up a chart to be placed in the bathroom as it is everyone's last stop at night before bed. The chart will show the number of evenings remaining over the goal period which is set at two more weeks. Every evening the chart will remind the members of their goal. The next morning the chart can be marked off to indicate that personal prayers took place for each person.

At the end of the third week of the goal period the family gathers to consult again. Dad reports that the youngest child was at first very fidgety and easily distracted until Dad hit upon the idea of saving the story-book until after the prayers and explaining that the story was a reward for sitting so well during the prayers. On some occasions he read two stories if the child made a

Goal Sheet : PLAN OF ACTION

Goal Must be Specific Measurable Positive Realistic Achievable	Obstacles to Goal Accomplishment	Action Steps to Overcome Obstacles If you can't define the action steps then the goal is not specific enough. Specify a time when you intend to evaluate progress and reassess.	Target Date When I will Accomplish this Goal	Rewards
Reaching this goal will lead towards the following longer-range goal:	After evaluating your progress, list any further obstacles to goal accomplishment	List amended or additional action steps	Amend Target Date if necessary	List any additional rewards
		EVALUATION		

Describe here: strengths which have been recognized as a result of pursuing this goal

weaknesses which have been recognized and will need to be overcome special effort. He also suggests that the child could paste coloured stars onto his own part of the chart to increase his sense of enjoyment and achievement and that perhaps when the full chart was completed the child could be presented with a new story-book as a reward.

At the end of the four-week period regular morning and evening prayers are well under way. However, it will take time to establish this as a firm habit. Adjustments will have to be made when the family attends summer school for a week or if one of the members is staying away from home and cannot be part of the family routine. For the youngest child, this habit of regular prayer will be the only way of life he can remember and so he will continue to follow the practice of morning and evening prayer effortlessly throughout the rest of his life.

Of course, this is just an example. The subjects and methods of goal-setting are as numerous and diverse as the people who practise this important skill. The goal sheet on p.105 is one example of how goal-setting might be approached and progress recorded.

The Training of Children: Reward and Punishment

The purpose of this section is to demonstrate the value of the process of knowledge/volition/action and goal-setting as tools in the training process.

> Whensoever a mother seeth that her child hath done well, let her praise and applaud him and cheer his heart; and if the slightest undesirable trait should manifest itself, let her counsel the child and punish him, and use means based on reason, even a slight verbal chastisement should this be necessary. It is not, however, permissible to strike a child, or vilify him, for the child's character will be totally perverted if he be subjected to blows or verbal abuse.[10]

There are two aspects of training: reward (praise) and

punishment. Bahá'u'lláh states, 'That which traineth the world is Justice, for it is upheld by two pillars, reward and retribution.'[11] In another place He states that the foundation of the order of the world is firmly established through the glad tidings of the promise of reward and the warning of punishment.[12] Through reward and punishment, promise and warning, training takes place, whether of animals, adults or children.

A simple explanation of why animals behave as they do is the pleasure/pain concept – an animal seeks out those things that give pleasure and avoids those things that cause pain. Animal trainers make use of this. For example, a dog learns that if he presses a certain lever he will receive food, but if he presses another he will receive an electric shock. The dog quickly learns to press the correct lever.

In the human world training uses the tool of consultation and involves praise and applause, counselling and reason. The intention of the parent is to educate the child and NEVER to seek vengeance or to give vent to anger through the use of violence. Beating or abusing a child will certainly stop the child behaving in the undesired way for a time. However, it will not educate him towards a better behaviour and will actually become the cause of many other and greater problems. It will pervert the child's character, damaging self-esteem, trust and security. It will also teach him to resolve his own problems and express his own feelings through force and violence.

The purpose of training is to increase the child's knowledge through counselling and reasoning, to foster his volition to change his behaviour using praise, applause and mild chastisement, and to aid him to act in a new and better way. This process of knowledge, volition and action can be assisted by using goal-setting. Through consultation, parent and child can consider why a certain behaviour is undesirable and what the negative consequences of that behaviour are. The parent can help the child to discover and identify better ways of behaving. The new type of behaviour can be expressed as a personal goal of the child.

In rewarding the child for practising his new behaviour, it may be sufficient to give praise and applause to the extent that an effort is being made. In other cases, a more tangible or specific reward could be given. For example, if the older child keeps her room tidy for a month, her pocket money will be increased. On the other hand, if she fails to do this, her pocket money will be decreased. The child must make her own choice of reward or punishment and, by making this choice for herself, she will develop a greater sense of personal responsibility. Younger children need more immediate rewards and punishments: a month is an eternity to young children. Perhaps the little one has been asked to put his books onto the shelf before bedtime. If he puts the books away, he will be read a bedtime story. If he doesn't put them away he will have no story.

Rewarding and punishing 'in kind' is a well-established principle. In the Bible the story is told about a servant who, being faithful and responsible to a small degree, was rewarded by having that responsibility to a greater degree. Conversely, if he did not fulfil expectations, then even that which he had would be taken from him. The same principle works for children. If the child appreciates, strives for and preserves something which is of value she will be given more of that valuable thing. On the other hand, if she fails to value it and strive for it, it will be denied her. The key point is that the object must be something of value – the child must learn to value it and deserve it or she will lose it. A similarity is that, to the extent that a person strives to master and to deserve a virtue, he or she will be rewarded by attaining it; if a person fails to appreciate that virtue, even what little he or she has will be lost. Therefore, it is ideal to reward or punish 'in kind'.

Whatever we give as a reward must be of real value and, of course, what we deny should also be of value. We should beware, however, of using food as a reward or a punishment. Research has indicated that where food is consistently offered as a reward to children, those children may grow up to continue rewarding themselves with food to such an extent that severe eating disorders may arise. Similarly, children who are denied food may, as they become independent, compensate for such earlier denial by eating vast quantities. Whilst for a young child the occasional sweet is acceptable, it must be given sparingly.

It is helpful to have a mental list of suitable rewards – and of suitable punishments – for each age of child so that a quick response to situations can be made. Rewards can include cuddles, games, stories, an occasional sweet, walks, etc. for younger children; and pocket money, trips, entertainment and, especially, increased independence or responsibility for older children. The aim of training is eventually to make the child an independent, self-determining adult, so one result of increased attainment should be increased responsibility and increased independence. Although material rewards have their place, they can only be viewed as a means to an end. The greatest reward of all is to secure the good-pleasure of the Lord. This is why the praise and pleasure of the parent is such an important aspect of training and why 'Abdu'l-Bahá has stated that it is the responsibility of children to secure the good-pleasure of their parents.[13] Having established this need in the heart of the child, the parents are able to step back and show that beyond their pleasure lies the all-important pleasure of God.

This 'stepping back' is important to the approaching maturity of the child because eventually the pleasure of

God must become the sole determinant of behaviour. Such must become the child's steadfastness that he will continue to follow the path of God even though his friends, his family, even the very heavens and earth arise against him.

There are many pointers which the parent can bear in mind in the training and discipline of the child.

1. Consult with the child. Through reasoning, show him the negative consequences of inappropriate behaviour and the desirability of the expected behaviour. Whenever possible, the child must be helped to understand the reasons for himself.

2. Formulate family standards and rules so that the child knows what is expected of him. It is not just to punish a child for something of which he is ignorant.

3. Do not expect too much from the child. It is unrealistic to expect a baby not to play with ornaments which are within reach. It is unrealistic to keep a child up for hours after his usual bedtime and expect him to behave well. In particular, do not expect something that you, yourself, do not practise. If you swear, it is probable that your child will also.

4. Do not expect too little of the child. Your child should be showing constant progress. You won't know the capacity of your seven-year-old child by observing other seven-year-olds. Your child is unique and capable of continual progress at his own level. Encourage him but don't push him.

5. Prepare the child for what you expect. Tell the toddler that it will be bedtime soon and he can have only a little more play before then. When you walk the five-

year-old to school, tell him that soon he will be able to walk alone. Teach him the skills he will need for the future. Don't tell the child it is time to dress himself without also teaching him to do up buttons, tie shoelaces and so forth.

6. Avoid problems. Know where your child is, and with whom he is playing, to avoid negative influences. Provide an environment that is safe, can take reasonable wear and tear and which is easily ordered. Children need good access to the things they use so that they won't disrupt the household. Things like tooth brushes and towels must be easily accessible; then the child can also put things away after using them. If he has access to cloths, sponges, brooms and so forth, he is better able to keep things clean and tidy.

7. Be consistent as much as possible. If you set bedtime at 8 o'clock, make sure it is acted on, or the child will see that you are not serious and will do as he likes. If you say 'no', but repeatedly give in to the child's complaining, you teach him to complain and to disobey.

8. Anticipate and avoid conflict if children are not ready to deal with it in a successful way. If two toddlers are about to come to blows over possession of a toy, step in with another toy. When the children are ready, you can teach them about sharing.

9. Distract children from undesirable behaviour. There is not time to make every situation a learning experience, neither are children always mature enough to handle some situations. If the baby is heading towards the fish bowl, redirect him to another activity. If he is heading for a tantrum, divert him

with a funny game. If the children are fighting over which game to play, ask them to help you with your chores.

10. Offer choices. Tell the grizzling child that he can grizzle in his room while he reads a book or he can sit with the family in the lounge if he will stop grizzling. He can eat part of his vegetables or he can eat all of his vegetables and then have dessert. He can sleep in late in the morning and prepare his own breakfast and wash the dishes used, or he can breakfast with the family. The child then becomes responsible for his own behaviour.

11. Negotiate with the child. Offer to tidy his room if he will water the garden. Agree to help him with a project if he will help with your chores.

12. Explain in advance the consequences or punishments of his failure to do what is asked. Explain that if the child has not finished his homework he will not be able to take part in an outing. If he loses his shoes, he will go barefoot until the family can afford new shoes. If he tears his clothes climbing a tree, he must mend them.

13. Be clear whether you are asking the child to do something or telling him to do it. Do you mean 'do you want to take the rubbish out?' or 'please take the rubbish out'. Don't offer a choice when you really intend him to do one thing in particular.

14. Establish a familiar order and routine so that good habits can be formed. A child will become familiar with the routine of dinner, bath, prayers, story, bed. If things take place in a different order or lack of time means that some are not completed, or if the place

where things are kept is changed frequently, it is hard
for the child to complete his duties.

15. Keep punishment for when it is needed. Children are
imperfect and can grow and achieve only at a given
rate. A certain degree of untidiness or squabbling can
be tolerated. Decide what is most important and
introduce new expectations one at a time.

16. Be true to your word. If you tell a child to do
something, ensure that it is done. If you say that the
child will miss out on an activity if homework is not
completed, follow this through. Empty threats achieve
nothing and undermine your credibility.

17. Know when to ignore behaviour. If the child is
whining in order to get attention, wait until the
whining stops and then give the attention – otherwise
you teach him that the way to be noticed is to whine.

18. Don't humiliate or belittle the child. This does to his
spirit what a beating does to the body. The body will
get over the pain but the child's spirit will keep its
scars. Children are more motivated to progress when
they feel happy and worthy and see themselves as
possessing great capacity. If a child is told that he is
worthless then he sets this as a permanent limitation
which will prevent him from achievement.

19. Make sure the child realizes that, whilst his behaviour
may be blameworthy, the child himself is a very
worthy and lovable person with great capacity.

20. Be honest and frank with the child. Apologize
whenever it is owing; this will teach the child that it is
human to make mistakes, that it is not shameful to
acknowledge error and limitation. Make amends if
you have harmed someone. Demonstrate the true

meaning of humility, remorse and humble fellowship in your relations with your children.

21. Take the child into your confidence when appropriate. Tell him about your feelings of disappointment or frustration. When you are tired or irritable or non-accepting, explain how you are feeling and ask the child for help and support. This teaches care, consideration and acceptance of others.

22. When you just can't cope and are losing control, get away. Take the child to a friend to mind or, if really desperate, shut him safely in his room and be by yourself for a time until you have cooled down and gained control. If you need to, seek help from partner, family, community, Spiritual Assembly or expert advisor.

23. Use plenty of rewards: cuddles, smiles, games, stars on a chart and so forth. Your loving company is often the best reward. Reward achievement by giving greater responsibility and a corresponding degree of independence. When the young child has begun to dress himself, let him choose what he wants to wear. When the child is old enough to receive pocket money for his duties, let him begin making his own donations to the Faith.

24. Praise and applaud the child and encourage the family as a whole to value the achievement of its members. Continually call God to mind and make the child aware of God's pleasure towards those who follow His path.

25. When the child has behaved wrongly, help him to make amends. As far as possible, let the punishment reflect the crime. If the child has broken another child's toy, help him to repair it. If he has forgotten to

feed the dog, let him add to the dog's pleasure by taking it for walks. In all things encourage him to see the consequences of his actions, so that this knowledge will prevent him from repeating those acts. Teach him that if we are truly sorry and wish to change, we will be forgiven. Encourage him to pray and seek God's forgiveness.

Help the child to set goals for new behaviours, to monitor his own progress and pray for assistance. With reward and praise, surround him with assurances of your pleasure. In this way the child will grow to see himself as a worthy being, capable of infinite progress, and will have his feet set firmly upon the path of the knowledge and love of God.

7

The Education of Children

The Value and Station of Education

If a family is likened to a business, then the 'goods' it produces are children. Certainly there are many other wonderful by-products of a family if it operates according to Bahá'í principles, but its fundamental purpose is to bring forth one who will make mention of God.

Unless we are consciously and continually striving to educate our children then our families are like businesses with factories, staff, equipment, shareholders and board members but which fail to produce the goods for which they were created. In fact, such a family is far worse, for neglectful parents will be held responsible in the presence of God.

Bahá'ís believe that the procreation of children is the primary purpose of that relationship between a man and a woman which attains its true consummation in marriage.[1] The education of our children is therefore the most urgent and sacred task facing us.

Some Misconceptions about the Spiritual Education of Children

Some Bahá'í parents are cautious about the extent to which they should train their children in the Faith. Some have the belief that a child should be offered the choice of whether or not to become a Bahá'í only at the age of spiritual maturity, that is fifteen. However the fact is that the children of two Bahá'í parents are Bahá'ís in their own right. It is only when one parent is not a Bahá'í that the question is raised and this is a matter for the couple to determine through joint consultation. For a Bahá'í parent to fail in this matter is 'a sin' and 'an omission'.[2] The age of fifteen is the age when a child moves from being the over-all responsibility of the parent to being responsible for his or her own spiritual obligations of prayer, fasting, obeying the laws, etc. The fifteen-year-old is now a Bahá'í through his or her own will and volition, and this is the primary significance. However, a corollary of this is that in some cases the fifteen-year-old may choose to remove himself or herself from the Faith.

Some parents are reluctant to do what they see as 'forcing' their choice of religion onto the child and, ignorant of their true responsibilities, look at the age of fifteen as a time when the child can choose to study the Bahá'í Faith through the process of independent investigation. The effect of this is to starve the child spiritually through his or her most important formative years. A child is not able to make informed choices but he or she should not live in a total vacuum until that time is reached. It is as if a parent were to say, 'When my daughter grows up she may not wish to eat meat. She may wish to be a vegetarian or a vegan or even a fruitarian. Therefore I will not feed my daughter at all but wait until she is old enough to feed herself'.

The healthiest, most fruitful of trees are those that have been nurtured as young seedlings. By the time a plant reaches maturity it is too late to correct the defects. The consequences of neglecting the training of children are awesome:

. . . in this new cycle, education and training are recorded in the Book of God as obligatory and not voluntary. That is, it is enjoined upon the father and the mother, as a duty, to strive with all effort to train the daughter and the son, to nurse them from the breast of knowledge and to rear them in the bosom of sciences and arts. Should they neglect this matter, they shall be held responsible and worthy of reproach in the presence of the stern Lord.[3]

This, then, is the consequence of failure to educate our children. On the other hand is the glorious promise, the reward, that children trained in the Bahá'í way will:

- free themselves of human imperfections
- dedicate their lives to matters of great import
- undertake studies that will benefit mankind
- become mirrors disclosing the secrets of the universe

. . . and so carry forth an ever-advancing civilization as bearers of the name of Bahá'u'lláh.

The Classroom of the Home

Many people think of education as being an often unpleasant process that takes place for about ten or more years of childhood, usually in an institutionalized setting of classrooms, teachers, etc. Consequently, when we become Bahá'ís we may tend to think of the Bahá'í education of our children in a similar way.

Perhaps we wave them off to weekly children's classes in our local community and sigh with relief that we can give someone else the responsibility. If we are isolated believers we may despair of being able to fulfil our weighty responsibilities without the provision of community children's classes. A primary purpose of the final chapter of this book is to suggest practical and achievable methods of educating our children in the home – methods in which the least confident parent can succeed and which the children will enjoy.

'Abdu'l-Bahá often prefaced His talks and personal communications by enquiring if the other was happy. 'Are you happy? Are you happy? Are you happy?' Happiness makes us receptive to new ideas and fosters growth and education.

In *Paris Talks*, 'Abdu'l-Bahá says:

> In this world we are influenced by two sentiments. *Joy* and *Pain*.
>
> Joy gives us wings! In times of joy our strength is more vital, our intellect keener, and our understanding less clouded. We seem better able to cope with the world and to find our sphere of usefulness. But when sadness visits us we become weak, our strength leaves us, our comprehension is dim and our intelligence veiled. The actualities of life seem to elude our grasp, the eyes of our spirits fail to discover the sacred mysteries, and we become even as dead beings. [4]

Therefore the first condition to be established in the process of educating children is happiness, whether in the home or in a classroom. If our children find their education boring, time-wasting or generally unpleasant, they will come to have a negative association with the cause of such unpleasantness.

We must take responsibility for our own children, beginning in the home where by far the most important education takes place. This is the education that forms the foundation stone of all other learning. Children who are unable to attend children's classes are denied the opportunity to experience the tremendous unity which is a feature of our Bahá'í gatherings and they are unable to take advantage of the enormous wealth of knowledge, talent and ability which others bring to children's classes; but their true Bahá'í education must proceed, with their parents taking what must always be the overriding responsibility for them, in a loving and happy environment. And if the children are clean, cheerful and loving, what does it really matter if they can't recite the names of the Bahá'í months or sing Alláh-u-Abhá in three part harmony?

> A child that is cleanly, agreeable, of good character, well-behaved – even though he be ignorant – is preferable to a child that is rude, unwashed, ill-natured, and yet becoming deeply versed in all the sciences and arts.[5]

Obviously the ideal is that our children receive as broad an education as we can provide. If we are able to provide a thorough grounding in the principles and practice of religion in the home, if we support community children's classes by contributing our own unique talents and abilities whenever possible to make them a more enjoyable and richer experience for the children, if we support our children's school teachers so that the children will gain as much benefit as possible from their time at school, then we will certainly ensure that our children will be a 'new creation'.

The Value of the Example Set by Parents

One of the most important means of training children is through the force of example. The value of example is demonstrated in the unique station of 'Abdu'l-Bahá as the Perfect Man, the Exemplar who offered us the example and inspiration of His own life saying, 'Look at Me, follow Me, be as I am.'[6] For this reason Bahá'ís the world over treasure the stories of the life of 'Abdu'l-Bahá for what can be learned through His example. The greatest teaching takes place through the force of deeds rather than words.

The Guardian speaks of the value of example in the home:

> It is often difficult for us to do things because they are so very *different* from what we are used to, not because the thing itself is particularly difficult. With you, and indeed most Bahá'ís, who are now, as adults, accepting this glorious Faith, no doubt some of the ordinances, like fasting and daily prayer, are hard to understand and obey at first. But we must always think that these things are given to all men for a thousand years to come. For Bahá'í children who see these things practised in the home, they will be as natural and necessary a thing as going to church on Sunday was to the more pious generation of Christians. Bahá'u'lláh would not have given us these things if they would not greatly benefit us, and, like children who are sensible enough to realize their father is wise and does what is good for them, we must accept to obey these ordinances even though at first we may not see any need for them. As we obey them we will gradually come to see in ourselves the benefits they confer.[7]

It is right that children should be extremely grateful and respectful towards their parents for this training by example. If we, as one generation of parents, exert a mighty effort to order our lives in a Bahá'í way – observing daily prayer, fasting, reading the Writings, giving to the Fund, holding regular firesides – then our children will do these things naturally. If we make a mighty effort to live the life, rectify our characters, purify our inner spiritual lives, then our children will conduct themselves similarly. In a sense we are helping them fight their own spiritual battles: through our tests, struggles and achievement we partly free our children from these burdens. We free them to devote their lives to even loftier objectives. This ensures the continual advancement and elevation of future generations.

Educating the Children: The Unique Privilege of Mothers

It is important that every aspect of our family life and, in particular, the education of children is soundly based upon known principles of the Faith. It is so easy to base our ideas on popular notions and misconceptions. This may have been excusable in earlier times when many people were illiterate and books unobtainable. The Bahá'í parent must be well-informed. 'Abdu'l-Bahá states:

> If the educator be incompetent, the educated will be correspondingly lacking.[8]

For this reason, the education of girls is of more importance because they are the mothers of the future. The mother is the primary educator of the child and if she is ignorant so, too, will be the child. However, except where circumstances necessitate one child receiving more attention, we are told that girls and boys should follow the same curriculum in order to promote the equality of the sexes.

One major principle of the Faith is, as we have seen, that the mother has the chief responsibility for the task of bringing up a Bahá'í child and that it is her unique privilege to create in the home such conditions as would be most conducive to the child's material and spiritual growth.

> Wherefore, O ye loving mothers, know ye that in God's sight, the best of all ways to worship Him is to educate the children and train them in all the perfections of humankind; and no nobler deed than this can be imagined . . .[9]

In fact, so great is the influence of the mother that we are told that

> . . . if the mother is a believer, the children will become believers too, even if the father denieth the Faith: while if

the mother is not a believer, the children are deprived of faith, even if the father be a believer convinced and firm. Such is the usual outcome, except in rare cases. [10]

Because our children are the most impressionable in the first few years of their lives, it is important that these years are used wisely. The child is like a branch which can be easily trained when it is fresh and green but, as it becomes older, can only be straightened by fire. For many parents of rebellious youth it is too late to change and redirect their children. When the Guardian was asked by some mothers if they should send their pre-schoolers to nursery school to allow them more time with their newborn infants, the reply was:

> With reference to the question of the training of children; given the emphasis placed by Bahá'u'lláh and 'Abdu'l-Bahá on the necessity for the parents to train their children while still in their tender age, it would seem preferable that they should receive their first training at home at the hand of their mother, rather than be sent to a nursery. Should circumstances, however, compel a Bahá'í mother to adopt the latter course, there can be no objection. [11]

This does not mean that mothers should, at every moment, be with their pre-schoolers; for if ever there is a time when women need support, relief and diversion, then this is it. What it does indicate is that parents should be very judicious in ensuring that the child is receiving all the training he or she requires from the mother and that other people are not exerting an undue influence upon the little one. Because the child is so impressionable, both the good and the bad will have a pronounced effect. If use is made of babysitters, creches and so forth, we should satisfy ourselves of the standards that our children will encounter.

When mothers are at home with young children it is important that they are supported in this greatest of all forms of worship. This is where the Bahá'í extended family can really come into play; for, in a sense, these children are all our children. Too often the mother in the home is seen as merely a 'housewife', who also looks after the kiddies in the gaps between waxing the floors and hanging out the washing. Indeed, when one stops to itemize all the roles that the housewife may be expected to fulfil in her day – chauffeur, nurse, home decorator, gardener, entertainer, cook, cleaner, painter, paperhanger, accountant, shopper, correspondent, errand girl – it's a wonder she has any time for the children at all!

The Bahá'í mother lives in a world which expects many things of a mother and at the same time treats motherhood as the lowest of all occupations. This astounding lack of appreciation for the priceless gift of parenting is reflected in an apparent belief that mothers do not work. When people describe their occupations it is common to hear a woman say that she is 'just a mother'. It is a sad comment on the values of our society that so many women believe that mothering has less value than other occupations and consequently prefer to describe their occupation as 'housewife', as if that were more acceptable. In fact, it is often a true description in terms of the priorities of the family and the relative distribution of the woman's workload. To overcome this attitude it has been suggested that women in the home should receive some payment; this would be a material reward from a material society for services rendered. In the Bahá'í view, spiritual values are greater than material values. The material world is an outer reflection of the spiritual world and never an end in itself. Whatever organization we intend to effect within our families, we must begin by isolating the spiritual values and principles and then ordering our material lives to reflect them.

This is another example of the extent to which the principles of the Faith are totally unlike current attitudes. We have to reverse completely the popular image of motherhood, to raise it to the greatest of all forms of worship, to encourage girls to become proficient mothers, to encourage mothers to take great pleasure in their role and to view it as a great privilege, to demonstrate our belief in the sacred task of childrearing by surrounding families with love and support. It is all too easy for us to pay lip-service to these values yet still cast the mother into those traditional roles of full-time cook/cleaner, etc.

At the same time, motherhood should not be an all-consuming occupation. Every woman is the recipient of many divinely-ordained talents and abilities which should not have to go into hibernation during the period of motherhood. To expect a person to spend all day, every day within four walls with only a pre-schooler for company, with none of the payrises or promotions which indicate appreciation or worth in the outside world, and with no holidays, no refresher courses or extension courses, and to expect all this for seven days a week, probably for a decade or more, is to place a tremendous strain upon that person. Furthermore, Bahá'í women are encouraged to involve themselves in society at large and they have a particular role in establishing world peace.

These are the challenges which each Bahá'í family will have to meet as it works to reconcile the requirements of Bahá'í mothering and being a Bahá'í woman with the pressures and expectations placed upon the 'simple house-wife' by television, magazines, radio, etc. The Bahá'í mother must strive to demonstrate the reality of Bahá'í principles in her own life, to show forth the evidences of equality, and to demonstrate the high station of mother-hood and the ability and integrity of Bahá'í women.

> But while this principle of equality is true, it is likewise true that woman must prove her capacity and aptitude, must show forth the evidences of equality. She must . . . prove by her accomplishments that her abilities and powers have merely been latent.[12]

We must treat our working hours in as professional a way as does the rest of the workforce. We cannot allow ourselves to while away the hours window shopping or visiting friends for endless cups of coffee. We cannot afford to spend hours watching television or browsing through magazines or entertaining an endless stream of casual visitors.

Naturally a Bahá'í is extremely courteous and hospitable, but not at the expense of her child's needs or the requirements of managing a home. Our families must come first and the needs of the community at large second. If we have a strong and spiritually dynamic family we will be enabled as a result to give more and more energy to the service of mankind. If we live our lives in this way we will gradually become a source of education and enlightenment but the change must begin with us. We can't look to our husbands or friends or community to make the changes for us.

We can timetable our days, making provision for taking the baby for a walk and popping in on the elderly lady down the road at the same time, helping out at Bahá'í children's classes, teaching the Faith, making time for regular exercise, family shopping, playing with the older children after school, having a quiet lunch with one's husband or taking the children to the library. Our time with our young families is really so very short and there is always so much to do. We must order our lives and strive to excel in what we do.

The Father as Educator

While the mother is the primary educator of the child, this by no means relegates the father to a role of merely overseeing. As the child grows the father is able to become more and more actively involved in the education of his child. Indeed, his involvement is crucial to a balanced upbringing, for just as the mother is strong in some particular qualities, so the father will be strong in others. This is not just a reference to the innate qualities of men and women. One partner may have a deep knowledge and love of the Writings to communicate; the other may have a great love and rapport for humanity. One may be a gifted musician, the other a talented writer. Each parent can communicate that love and enthusiasm and assist the children to develop similar qualities latent within themselves in such a way that the children will become sources of enlightment and joy to their fellowmen. It is said that opposites attract and it is true of many marriages that we often seek qualities within our partners which will balance and complement our own. Seldom do we wish to duplicate qualities which we already possess. As a result, a woman who is extremely compassionate may marry a man who is extremely just and these qualities become a good balance for one another. If the father plays no part in the education of his children they will grow up with only the example of extreme compassion and consequently in situations requiring justice they will be at a loss.

Bahá'í fathers, too, are faced with a society which has extremely different values from those they are trying to embody. While in many places the situation is gradually changing, it is still the case that in most societies the father generally has little involvement with his children apart from earning their keep, playing the odd spot of sport with them and appearing when a bit of 'real' discipline is required. It is feared that too much affection will do permanent damage to impressionable young minds so dad must content himself with a slap on the back or a tweak of the ear. The only emotion he is allowed to show is pride when the home team wins or when his country's nationalism is appealed to. Contrast this with 'Abdu'l-

Bahá who kissed and prayed and wept and laughed, had a passionate love for all children and an unbounded love and affection for His own dear Father. The Bahá'í father is not afraid to pray with such depth of feeling that those who hear him are moved by the very sound. He will take his newborn infant aside in the presence of businesslike hospital staff and whisper a prayer of profound significance into his child's ear. He forthrightly acknowledges to his workmates that he will make no decision on a certain subject without first consulting his wife. Bahá'í women are encouraged to meet and support one another in applying the principles of the Faith to their own lives. Bahá'í men find that together they, too, are able to support each other in similar ways, suggesting to the rest of us ways in which we can assist them to fulfil their roles more readily.

The Three Kinds of Education

But education is of three kinds: material, human and spiritual. Material education is concerned with the progress and development of the body, through gaining its sustenance, its material comfort and ease. This education is common to animals and man.

Human education signifies civilization and progress – that is to say, government, administration, charitable works, trades, arts and handicrafts, sciences, great inventions and discoveries and elaborate institutions, which are the activities essential to man as distinguished from the animal.

Divine education is that of the Kingdom of God: it consists in acquiring divine perfections, and this is true education; for in this state man becomes the focus of divine blessings, the manifestation of the words, 'Let Us make man in Our image, after Our likeness'. This is the goal of the world of humanity.[13]

The aim of parents in the education of their children is to

enable them to grow into independent, autonomous adults capable of providing for their own material, human and spiritual needs. At adulthood the individual becomes responsible for his or her own relationship with God. Everything he or she needs to know about becoming an independent person must be acquired by this time, although one's spiritual development is an infinite process. Obviously it is impossible to teach a child the sum total of human knowledge. What we must teach are the fundamental principles of human and divine life. We must teach the children to search out knowledge for themselves, to think about and process what they read, to apply that knowledge to their personal needs, to set sensible goals for themselves and to express those goals through action.

The first level – material knowledge – is no more than a lioness might teach her cubs: how to provide for the body's needs for food, shelter and health. This is partly taught at home and, ideally, partly within the school curriculum. In addition, 'Abdu'l-Bahá specifically stated that girls should study household management, the education of children, whatever would nurture the health of the body and its physical soundness and how to guard their children from disease. [14]

The second area, human knowledge, is also provided by the state school system. However, a knowledge of the Bahá'í Writings on these aspects gives us a better perspective of the relationship of human knowledge to the divine life and offers criteria whereby we may determine how effectively knowledge is being applied. In areas which seem inadequate we can make alternative provision for our children.

The following selections from the Writings apply to human education:

> Teach them to dedicate their lives to matters of great import . . . [15]

. . . inspire them to undertake studies that will benefit mankind.[16]

Give them the advantage of every useful kind of knowledge.[17]

Unto every father hath been enjoined the instruction of his son and daughter in the art of reading and writing . . .[18]

. . . it is enjoined upon the father and mother, as a duty, to strive with all effort to train the daughter and the son, to nurse them from the breast of knowledge and to rear them in the bosom of sciences and arts.[19]

Let them share in every new and rare and wondrous craft and art.[20]

Bring them up to work and strive, and accustom them to hardship.[21]

. . . each child must be taught a profession, art, or trade . . .[22]

It is incumbent upon each child to know something of music . . .[23]

Train your children from their earliest days to be infinitely tender and loving to animals.[24]

[teach girls] household management, the education of children, and whatever especially applieth to the needs of girls . . .[25]

Of divine education 'Abdu'l-Bahá states that it

. . . is true education; for in this state man becomes the focus of divine blessings the manifestation of the words 'Let Us make man in Our image, and after Our likeness'. This is the goal of the world of humanity.[26]

This is the area of education upon which we as parents must continually focus if we are to rear children who are staunch and firm in the Faith. This, of all the kinds of education, is the one for which God will hold us accountable, the one for which neglectful parents 'shall be held responsible and worthy of reproach in the presence of the stern Lord',[27] a neglect which is 'a sin unpardonable'.[28]

The last chapter of this book will explore the requirements of divine education and suggest practical methods to implement it which parents can employ.

8

Divine Education

An Eternal Process

Divine education is the goal of the world of humanity, the process of growing in the knowledge and love of God. As the knowledge of God is infinite, so too is the process of divine education. However, the Bahá'í Writings suggest both a method and an order of importance in this process of educating our children. Some aspects of divine education are described as being 'of paramount importance', which 'must precede all else', which are 'absolutely indispensible', and which should take place 'continually'. Specific responsibilities are given to the father and to the mother. We are encouraged to follow methods used by 'Abdu'l-Bahá.

As far as possible the ordering of the subjects of this chapter reflect the priorities and employ the methods suggested in the Bahá'í Writings, selections from which are quoted below.

The Oneness of God, His Laws and the Fear of God

That which is of paramount importance for the children, that which must precede all else, is to teach them the oneness of God and the Laws of God. For lacking this, the fear of God cannot be inculcated, and lacking the fear of God an infinity of odious and abominable actions will spring up, and sentiments will be uttered that transgress all bounds . . .'[1]

This is a knowledge which both mother and father can teach from the earliest of ages:

The father:

> The father must always endeavour to educate his son and to acquaint him with the heavenly teachings. He must give him advice and exhort him at all times, teach him praiseworthy conduct and character, enable him to receive training at school and to be instructed in such arts and sciences as are deemed useful and necessary. In brief, let him instil into his mind the virtues and perfections of the world of humanity. Above all he should continually call to his mind the remembrance of God so that his throbbing veins and arteries may pulsate with the love of God.[2]

The mother:

> . . . the mother must continually call God to mind and make mention of Him, and tell of His greatness, and instil the fear of Him in the child, and rear the child gently, in the way of tenderness, and in extreme cleanliness. Thus from the very beginning of life every child will be refreshed by the gentle waftings of the love of God and will tremble with joy at the sweet scent of heavenly guidance. In this lieth the beginning of the process; it is the essential basis of all the rest.[3]

This, then, is the beginning of the process of educating our children, the essential basis of our success as parents and of the eternal happiness of our children. It requires of both parents one thing in particular, something which those of us who have only recently as adults accepted the Faith may find a bit daunting: we are asked to call God continually to mind and to make mention of Him. In a world where God has become a 'Sunday' topic at best and completely forgotten at worst, we must begin the process of first raising our own consciousness of the nearness of God and then expressing that awareness to our children. It is a goal which must be tackled one step at a time as we introduce into our own lives a regular pattern of reciting the daily obligatory prayers, praying and reading the Writings morning and evening, meditating and studying, intoning the Greatest Name and participating in community affairs. As we allow God into our lives more and more often, and strive to see the face of the Beloved in every aspect of creation, we can share our love of God with our children so that from their earliest years this love may become a deep and precious part of their being.

The very youngest child is capable of responding to the knowledge that a beautiful flower or a tiny kitten is part of God's creation. As the small child lies in his mother's arms whilst she prays or recites from the Writings or sings the verses of God, he is aware of a sense of tranquillity and contentment and joy. As the children gather around their parents in warm companionship and unity to share family prayers, they respond in their hearts to the spirit of the moment. As older children go to their parents for assistance with specific problems, they will learn Bahá'í principles and solve their problems through consultation. In every moment of beauty, in every moment of difficulty and in every moment of remembrance the thoughts of these children will naturally turn to their Creator as a result of the continuous endeavours of their parents.

In addition to seeing all beauty and happiness and honour and greatness as an emanation from God, children will learn also to fear the justice and punishment of God as He seeks to guide and educate them.

In explaining the fear of God to children, there is no objection to teaching it as 'Abdu'l-Bahá so often taught everything, in the form of parables. Also the child should be made to understand that we don't fear God because He is cruel, but we fear Him because he is just and, if we do wrong and deserve to be punished, then in His justice He may see fit to punish us.[4]

One way in which children are able to understand the punishment of God might be in helping to train a young puppy or even by observing the way in which a younger brother or sister is trained. For example, a child can appreciate that a puppy should not be allowed to jump up to the table in order to get at food; certainly the puppy should be fed but in a suitable way. The child understands that the parent does not smack the puppy to be cruel but to train it. The toddler must be trained not to tear the pages of the book so that he and others can continue to enjoy reading it. If, having learned that tearing books is not right, the toddler continues to behave this way, the older child will appreciate that a gentle but educative punishment might be necessary.

Obedience to Parents

The parents must exert every effort to rear their offspring to be religious, for should the children not attain this greatest of adornments, they will not obey their parents, which in a certain sense means that they will not obey God. Indeed, such children will show no consideration to anyone, and will do exactly as they please.[5]

At a time when many parents uphold the concept of permissive parenting in a belief that freedom for the children will make them happier and teach independence and responsibility, it can be difficult at first to realize that true freedom lies in submission to God. On the other hand, authoritarian parenting is also unsuccessful. In this world we are subject to both material and spiritual laws which are a reflection of God's Will for man on earth; we recognize that no matter how determined or intelligent or powerful we may be, we can never hope to change these laws. Rather, our only hope for happiness is to recognize these laws and to operate within them, to obey them.

Children are able to recognize and accept the necessity of obedience to God through both experience and parable. For example, most children find the idea of flight very appealing and are attracted by the idea of being able to move effortlessly and with absolute freedom. However, they are also able to recognize that flight is possible only when the laws of gravity, aerodynamics and so on are accounted for and worked within: a glider or a bird appears to fly effortlessly because it is operating within physical laws. These examples teach the child that recognition and understanding of laws and obedience to them is the only source of growth, progress and advancement; for with each decade humankind now discovers more and more effective methods of flight. By obeying laws, humanity has achieved greater freedom!

The child can also see in the helplessness of a young animal its absolute dependence upon the mother and the infinite love and care she shows to the young one. The child acknowledges the superior knowledge of the mother, that her concern is only for the young one's welfare – its protection, education and gradual independence. If the mother were to give the young animal its 'freedom', the child is readily able to predict the outcome and to see that the best interests of a child, too, are in submission to mother and father and, beyond them, to God Himself.

Whenever situations arise in which the child is required to be obedient, it is important – when the parent has the time and if the circumstances allow – to explain in a reasoning fashion to the child why a certain behaviour is required.

Although as adults we are expected to show unqualified obedience to the laws of God, we are also expected to strive to know God and to understand the teachings. Once we understand, that in itself further strengthens our obedience. Through explanation and reasoning, the child will gradually come to accept the necessity of obedience.

Whilst at first the child will obey because he seeks the pleasure and assistance of his parents, gradually he should be encouraged to do so for the sake of God. This will take place when the parents, in explaining to the child the reason for a certain behaviour, relate it to the Will of God. For example, they may instruct the child to feed the puppy, stating that God wishes children to be exceedingly kind and merciful to animals. The older the child, the more he can be taught on any subject according to his needs. This is a very important part of the education of children which, rather than taking place at some specified time of the week in formal lessons, becomes a part of the day-to-day life of the family.

The Importance of Prayer

> The believers, particularly the young ones, should, therefore, fully realize the necessity of praying. For prayer is absolutely indispensable to their inner spiritual development . . .[6]

Our children cannot dispense with prayer if they are to develop spiritually; it is as vital for children to pray as it is for adults. Just as children need food to develop their physical bodies, so they need prayer to develop the spirit. Children are particularly encouraged to pray for their parents using one of several prayers revealed for the purpose.

At first the young baby will lie in her mother's arms during prayer, enjoying the spirit generated from this. As she learns the elements of speech she will be able to say 'Alláh-u-Abhá' and later to memorize a line or two from a

children's prayer, maybe just the words 'O God, guide me
. . .' At about the age when children can speak in short
sentences they will feel especially proud to have their own
prayer book. This may be merely a notebook into which
the lines of prayers which the child has learned are entered,
perhaps beautified by some pictures cut from magazines or
greeting cards and pasted in. She will also feel very proud
that she is expected to take part regularly in family prayer.
Bedtime prayers, prior to the afternoon nap and the
evening sleep, will become an enjoyable part of the daily
routine and will be looked forward to with anticipation.
The child will also appreciate being able to take part in
community prayers at Feasts or Holy Days and so forth
and this will encourage a feeling of responsibility and
appreciation of the significance of prayer.

When older children first become Bahá'ís the habit of
regular prayer needs thoughtful encouragement and reward.
A chart can be made by parent and child together and
decorated attractively, its purpose being that the child will
receive a star for every day over a given period when he or
she remembers to pray. If the child likes, the chart could
be displayed in an important place in the home. In addition
to the reward of stars, the child could receive his or her
first 'real' prayer book from the parents, perhaps suitably
inscribed and presented, on the attainment of the agreed
number of stars.

Some Bahá'í prayers have been set to music and are
available on tapes and records. The receipt of such a tape as
a gift could inspire the child to memorize and use the
prayers or could be a fitting reward for the child's
perseverance in praying or memorizing.

An exciting way for children to memorize prayers,
especially if they enjoy music, is to put prayers or parts of
prayers to music and, with any assistance you may be able
to give, to tape the results. This can quickly build up to a

whole tape full of Bahá'í prayers. If the quality is up to it, the tape may be copied and shared with others.

Individual prayers can be 'illuminated'. The child can copy the prayer carefully onto a card (at this stage it may even be photocopied to give as gifts) and then work a decorated border around it, perhaps using gold and silver felt tip pens and poster paints.

Older children will really appreciate the responsibility of being asked to select prayers for Feast or Holy Day programmes and to present them after careful preparation and practice. The more our children are able to be involved in family and community devotions and Holy Days, the greater will be their enjoyment and commitment and the more enriched will be the community. These children will also be a source of inspiration to children newly entering the Faith.

The greatest encouragement to regular prayer, however, will be the example of the parents. If the family comes together each morning for family prayer, if parents continually foster the observance of individual or family evening prayer and if the parents themselves practice regular personal prayer this will have a great effect.

Knowledge of the Bahá'í Writings

When the children are ready for bed, let the mother read or sing them the Odes of the Blessed Beauty, so that from their earliest years they will be educated by these verses of guidance.[7]

It is also highly praiseworthy to memorize the Tablets, divine verses and sacred traditions.[8]

Reading the Writings is a source of knowledge and guidance. It also has a mystical effect upon the soul; even saying one of the Hidden Words or reading other Writings over a sleeping child will have an influence. Another benefit of regular exposure to the Word of God is that over the entire period of childhood the child will eventually commit to memory a remarkable number of sacred verses which will be instantly available when the need arises.

Of course, this knowledge is only of use to the child if it is transmuted into action. Through day-to-day discussions arising out of routine incidents, such knowledge can be practically applied. For example, if the child is familiar with the Writings about kindness to animals, this can be referred to when a stray kitten comes to the door. A quotation on freedom from prejudice can be applied when a child from a minority race arrives at school. Verses on world peace can be applied to a disagreement with a friend. These are just the average daily happenings which typically surface amongst children and which the parent routinely handles anyway. What is suggested here requires no extra input from the parent; rather, it involves making otherwise insignificant events into real learning experiences. These are learning experiences in several different ways:

- Recalling the memorized verse reinforces the memory.

- The words assume a reality for the child because they are seen to apply to everyday life and to offer real guidance to everyday problems and experiences. They are seen as an important source of wisdom to the child and therefore to be valued.

- The habit is established, to be continued into adult life, of going to the Writings on a regular basis for guidance and inspiration.

For older children the order can be reversed: rather than learning a verse which will be applied later as a relevant situation arises, children can begin to seek out those

Writings which apply to existing needs. For example, if the child is troubled by a situation at school which seems unjust, he can be assisted to search out a relevant quotation for study and application. This is preparing the child for adulthood when he will be expected to investigate independently and to apply the Writings. A concordance on the Bahá'í Writings is extremely useful for this. These books contain alphabetical lists of themes and a list of sources from the Writings which apply to each theme. The child first needs to isolate some 'key words' which relate to the subject he wishes to study. In the case of injustice at school, the key words may be justice, injustice or authority.

Requiring less assistance from the parent as time goes by, the child can research themes from the Writings which are relevant to his needs and then, perhaps in consultation with a parent, prayerfully apply the guidance derived. The parents may even wish this to become a valuable weekly exercise in Bahá'í studies for the child, and consequently may establish an enjoyable and regular routine of after-school study. Of course, this will only succeed if the child finds such an activity rewarding, so careful consideration needs to be given to how this can be achieved.

Many of the suggestions made with respect to encouraging regular prayer can be applied to reading the Writings too: contributing to family and community devotions, making illuminated quotation cards, using the 'chart and star' reward system, recording quotations in an attractively decorated notebook, receiving a gift of a book of Bahá'í Writings, setting verses to music and taping them, etc. This is another crucial area in which the example of the parents will have a big effect on the child. If our children observe that we routinely seek guidance for our daily lives in the Holy Writings, they will be far more likely to follow suit. Regular recourse to the Writings during family consultation, perhaps encouraging the children to assist in finding the relevant quotations, will greatly reinforce such an attitude.

Observance of Feasts and Holy Days

Bahá'í children can often feel at a disadvantage when the majority of children in their schools and communities have widely observed and accepted Holy Days. They can feel as if the Bahá'í Holy Days are not quite 'real'. This is not just because of the 'fun' and 'goodies' of Christmas and Easter but also because of the inferred significance of these days: our children can think that because so much activity and excitement is generated by the birth of Christ then the birth of Bahá'u'lláh is perhaps not as important. They may find it difficult to appreciate the significance of the Bahá'í Holy Days and also miss out on what can be warm, unified and moving family and community observances. It is very important that we begin now to establish our Holy Days as vital events of the Bahá'í calendar. Whenever possible we should seek leave of absence from our occupations and request the children's approved absence from their schools and, as individuals or communites, we should hold befitting celebrations or commemorations for each Holy Day. These occasions also serve to bind the community together, to give a feeling of unity and a sense of purpose.

Children have a great sense of occasion and enjoy the planning and anticipation that are part of such events. There are so many ways in which they can contribute – in the consultation required to plan the occasion, making suggestions for programming, taking part in devotions, contributing stories or songs or pictures about the occasion, cleaning the house beforehand, preparing decorations or food. Not only will this make their Faith come alive for them but many an adult will be amazed at how much the children have enriched the Faith for them too.

Contributing to the Fund

As a result of the education which our children are receiving at our hands they will see that the real world is the world of the spirit, that this material world is subservient to it and will soon be abandoned in the path towards God. Giving to the Fund is a demonstration of this knowledge. We give of our material means that through this the institutions promoting the spiritual life may be strengthened. The children will grow to recognize that all things come from God and that He has promised to provide for our needs. This knowledge can be imparted through the example of the parents and through teaching by analogy.

Some parents may like to approach giving to the Fund as a united family effort, emphasizing the aspects of universal participation. Through family consultation, goals can be adopted which give each member, no matter the age or material means, some responsibility for the family's contribution. This may be considered a good context in which to introduce some system of 'pocket money' because it puts into a spiritual context the matter of material remuneration for services from the earliest age. For example, the five-year-old, in consultation with the rest of the family, could be given responsibility for feeding the dog each day and for keeping his own room tidy, and in return his services might be acknowledged by the receipt of pocket money. Again through consultation, the child could set himself a regular goal of placing a small amount of that pocket money in the family 'donations' box. Some children may even appreciate a receipt from the treasurer as an acknowledgement that their contribution is

as worthy as that of an adult. From time to time, as in
cases when a special or urgent call for funds is made, the
family jointly may decide to make some special sacrifice in
order to contribute. At such times even the youngest child
can respond generously and sacrificially in some way and
experience that special joy which comes with sacrifice.

The principle of sacrifice can be illustrated through
analogy. We are asked to be like the fountain which
continually gives of itself and is replenished. In autumn the
tree gives its fruit for our enjoyment and yet, having been
depleted, grows even greater and more fruitful in the
season that follows. The oak tree loses its acorns but,
come spring, many new oaks come to life as a result. The
child will be able to identify many examples of the
principle of sacrifice in the world around him and to
realize that its nature is fundamental to the world of
creation.

Children will appreciate having the results of their
contributions 'personalized' in a meaningful way. For
example, the family could maintain a chart illustrating the
amount of the family contribution as it creeps towards the
set goal; perhaps the children could have the responsibility
for maintaining it. The progress of a particular travel-
teaching team sponsored by the family could be followed
or the family could adopt and correspond with a pioneer.

These are just a few ideas which may be helpful. Each
family will have particular ways of educating the children
about the Fund according to member's needs and resources.

Children and Teaching the Faith

We have already considered the necessity for the child to
develop a sound knowledge of the Writings for his or her
own instruction and enlightenment, and have stressed the
need for this knowledge to become the cause of growth,

development and the acquisition of divine virtues. This is the first requisite of teaching, as Shoghi Effendi wrote:

> Not by the force of numbers, not by the mere exposition of a set of new and noble principles, not by an organized campaign of teaching – no matter how worldwide and elaborate in its character – not even by the staunchness of our faith or the exaltation of our enthusiasm, can we ultimately hope to vindicate in the eyes of a critical and sceptical age the supreme claim of the Abhá Revelation. One thing and only one thing will unfailingly and alone secure the undoubted triumph of this sacred Cause, namely, the extent to which our own inner life and private character mirror forth in their manifold aspects the splendour of those eternal principles proclaimed by Bahá'u'lláh.[9]

In this vital sense, the parent who carefully and lovingly trains the child and shapes his character in conformity with the principles of the Faith, is laying down the essential foundation of a successful teacher. A child so trained will attract others by his excellence and will be outstanding amongst his peers, exemplifying all the virtues of courtesy, kindness, cleanliness and fairness. He will greet others with pleasant courtesy and be concerned about their happiness. He will hospitably care for their needs and make his home their own. He will share what he has and treat others equitably. He will dress neatly, cleanly and moderately. He will avoid the frivolous amusements popular amongst his peers but associate freely with people of all races and religions in a true spirit of fellowship and, in so doing become a centre of attraction for sincere and searching souls.

> Just because you are children does not mean you cannot serve the Faith, and teach it, by your example and by the way you let people see that you are better and more intelligent than most other children.[10]

The child who has developed a true Bahá'í character now stands in need of knowledge in order to guide and instruct others.

> Wherefore must the loved ones of God, be they young or old, be they men or women, each one according to his capabilities, strive to acquire the various branches of knowledge, and to increase his understanding of the mysteries of the Holy Books, and his skill in marshalling the divine proofs and evidences.[11]

Children who are able to attend regular Bahá'í children's classes are very fortunate for here they will study the Writings of the Faith, become familiar with the principles and know the quotations from the Writings which support those principles. By doing so, they will be able in their teaching work to give the pure Word. In the children's classes they will also be able to study ways and means of presenting the Faith. As previously considered, parents too can develop in the child a sound knowledge of the Writings of the Faith – foster the regular reading of the Sacred Writings, encourage memorization of verses and in day-to-day life demonstrate the practical application of divine teachings. We have considered a method whereby, in the absence of regular children's classes, children can pursue a regular study programme in a way which has direct practical application to their needs and interests. These are all an assistance to children in their preparation for teaching the Faith.

This preparation through character development and the acquisition of knowledge can be expressed in the formulation of specific teaching goals and objectives. For example, the release of a new teaching plan from the Local or National Spiritual Assembly can be the subject of family consultation as the family responds by formulating its own practical teaching plan and goals. This would employ the principle of universal participation and allow every member to make a valuable contribution. An example of the sort of goals which a child might adopt are as follows:

1. *Each one of the friends must teach at least one soul a year*
   My aim is to teach my class teacher by treating him with obedience and respect and showing him what Bahá'ís are meant to be like.

2. *A vast increase in the number of believers*
   I will pray for the goals each day using the prayer 'O Lord! Open thou the door . . .' I will memorize that prayer.

3. *Hold a fireside in the home once every 19 days*
   I will ask a friend over to play at least once every nineteen days. I will treat him with hospitality and courtesy.

4. *Make a personal commitment to teach*
   I will try to find more opportunities in my daily life to teach the faith.

5. *Families can teach other families. Reach Maori and minority groups*
   I will make special friends with Maori children at school and maybe as a result our families can get together and get to know one another.

6. *Pray, using regular organized prayer sessions*
   Mum and I will have a special prayer session for the goals during each weekly Bahá'í study class.

7. *Form at least six Local Spiritual Assemblies in areas of substantial Maori population*
   I will write regularly to my friend Rawinia in Kaitaia and invite her to stay during the summer holidays.

Of course this is only an example. The type of plan which a child may formulate will depend on his or her age and capacity and preparation, on the support which the family members can offer one another and upon their resources. A family of musicians has a very useful gift in the teaching field, a family with a pool or barbeque area yet another, and the Bahá'í who is a good cook may find a special truth to the remark that the way to a man's heart is through his stomach. The child, too, will have special gifts and aptitudes which can be used to advantage in teaching. However, whatever principles the child may learn, whatever plans he or she may adopt, the words of the beloved Guardian should be a continual reminder to us both as parents and as individuals that only one thing will unfailingly secure the triumph of the Cause: the extent to which our own lives and character mirror divine qualities.

Children in Community Life

> How often have the children, through their songs and recitation of prayers during Feasts and other gatherings of the friends, added lustre and inspiration to the programme and created a true sense of belonging in the hearts of those present.[12]

So commented the Universal House of Justice in setting the goals of the Five Year Plan. We all recognize the truth of this observation from our own experiences. The community which fails to draw upon the talents of its children is depriving itself of a most valuable resource and denying the children an important way of serving others.

A common reason why many communities and parents restrict the involvement of children in community activities is that bored, restless and irritable children can be such a distraction for all concerned. This is an important problem which cannot be solved by either denying the participation of the children or by becoming resigned to the chaos and confusion which untrained children will cause. These problems can all be rectified by thoughtful and consistent training.

Children in the western world are becoming used to an increasing bombardment of external stimuli due to the high entertainment value of toys, television, video games and so on which offer instant rewards. Today's child is probably less likely than his father was to enjoy sitting on a river bank for hours in the hope of catching a fish. The skills of meditation and reflection – what a poet once described as 'time to stand and stare' – are not developed.

The qualities of patience, listening for understanding, reverence and self-discipline also need development. Children need assistance to recognize the subtle but powerful beauty of prayers and the Writings, to recognize and enjoy the fragrance of spirituality and unity. They require self-control and restraint and the ability to know at which times they should express themselves and at which times they should refrain.

Children are naturally very active beings and need to be trained to remain still for any period of time. Also, children new to the Faith may find the practice of prayer and reading the Writings rather strange and uninteresting at first and may lose interest quickly. However, at other times children do sit still and concentrate for quite lengthy periods – observe them when they are being read a favourite book or watching an exciting television programme. Such experiences are very pleasurable. One good way to begin this training is to include it as part of family prayer every day. For example, in the morning the parents can gather the children together, with the little ones in their laps. Even the youngest child can have his or her own prayer book to bring to this gathering. In this atmosphere of love, warmth and companionship each child can say a prayer or a few words of a prayer, feeling a sense of self-worth at this personal contribution. One child can have the responsibility for bringing a book of readings to the gathering each morning, perhaps *The Hidden Words*, and may even have the task of reading from it – just see what this will do for the child's reading ability! At first it may be reasonable to expect a child to sit quietly for only a minute or two. Soon this will become ten or twenty minutes, the time often required for the devotional portion of Feasts. The important aspects of this method of training are as follows:

- The practice must be regular; for example, this training can take place every morning or at bedtime, when the parent and child say prayers, sing a Hidden Word or prayer, or perhaps read from a Bahá'í children's book.

- The parents must expect a consistent level of behaviour, e.g. no talking, no wriggling, no walking out of the room. Such behaviour can be discouraged in a suitable way, perhaps by reasoning with an older child, who can understand the principles involved, or even a warning tap on the hand for very young children who cannot be reasoned with. This is an immediate punishment which, followed by an affectionate return to the parent's lap and resumption of the prayer, makes clear to the little one what his parents expect of him without causing a huge disruption. Whatever the method, some form of discipline must be used to achieve a consistent standard of behaviour – if you allow the child to giggle through today's prayers, he will try it again tomorrow. If you allow it tomorrow, he will wriggle around and try to get away until, seeing that you are not serious about training, he will eventually do what he likes.

- The child must be happy and find the whole experience

pleasurable. This is most important for if the child is happy he will behave well of his own accord. There are many different approaches a family can take to make their gatherings enjoyable; the following are but a few suggestions.

Music has a great effect upon the spirit, especially for children. As the family is rising and preparing for morning prayer some beautiful music can be played. In winter the family can gather around the fire or heater so that they can pray in comfort. Children enjoy making an occasion of activities. They may like to take responsibility for keeping fresh flowers in the room in which the family gathers, to place the Greatest Name or a portrait of 'Abdu'l-Bahá in a place of honour, to light incense, to protect the Holy Books in a special cloth which they have prepared for that purpose, or to be given the responsibility of passing out prayer books or selecting the Writings to be read. The purpose in this is not to suggest a form or ritual for any of these activities but rather to provide the children with suitable forms through which they can express their special feelings of respect, dignity, beauty and reverence.

The entire occasion should be one of love, harmony and unity so that the child is surrounded by happiness and contentment and affection. This is especially so if the child has required punishment; it's a pretty safe rule of thumb that to whatever extent a child requires punishment, he or she should be loved ten times more than that in general life.

Once children are accustomed to sitting still regularly for family prayers, they will be better prepared to attend community activities, sitting with the parents so that they are under proper supervision as long as this is necessary. Children should be expected to behave well only to the extent to which they have so far been trained. For some children this may be only five or ten minutes, at which time the parents could take turns at caring for their child in another room. It is very important not to expect more from a child than he is capable of, for then he is guaranteed to fail. The failure will disappoint him and make the whole experience unpleasant and one to be avoided whenever possible. Some special activities could be provided afterwards, as a reward for good behaviour at the gathering. The more successful you can help children to be by making sure they will succeed at what you ask of them, the more rewarding they will find it and the faster they can be trained.

In larger communities, the parents may choose to get together to devise a system which suits everyone's needs. Non-parents may happily get involved in such an activity, thereby relieving hard-working parents, learning a great deal themselves about children and contributing their own special skills and abilities. However, whatever the involvement and support of the larger community, the child remains the parents' responsibility.

The Nineteen Day Feast provides the most regular opportunity for the community to meet together. Children's activities can be held after the combined devotional portion of the Feast. It is good if the whole community can be together for at least a part of the Feast, even if for only five or ten minutes. The children can contribute their own, preferably practised, prayers and readings at this time. A child not able to last through this period can be quietly withdrawn by a parent until such time as the remainder of the children withdraw to begin their Feast activities.

Perhaps as part of the social portion of the Feast the children could share work done during their activity session, present a short play or story or sing songs. They could have the opportunity to prepare and serve the supper. During their activities they could prepare recommendations to be shared with the full community at the next month's Feast and in this way feel that they are a valued part of the community. The aim should be to enable the children to participate fully throughout the entire Feast without needing to be withdrawn, because Feasts and Holy Days are for the benefit of the entire community and not just the adults.

Feasts are not the only community events which children can beneficially attend. Unity Feasts, Holy Day celebrations, prayer gatherings and firesides, if held at suitable hours and not demanding more of the children than they can successfully accomplish, will be greatly enriched by allowing for some contribution from children. A child will only learn to behave responsibly when he or she is given responsibility. These Bahá'í children of ours, trained towards the attainment of excellence, will delight their fellow Bahá'ís and attract and inspire others, if only we train them wisely and give them the opportunity.

Bahá'í Children's Classes

At present, our children's education is very compartmentalized – they attend state schools for 'human' education and depend on their parents for 'divine' education. A relatively few children are fortunate enough also to attend organized Bahá'í children's classes. At some time in the future these Bahá'í classes will become the only schools our children will attend, and divine and human knowledge will be taught hand-in-hand. At the present time, however, Bahá'í education is in its infancy and many parts of the world have yet to develop children's classes. As we develop these classes, lend them our active support and encourage our children to attend regularly, we are hastening the day when they will become the true schools of our communities. Not for us, yet, the luxury of waving our children off to classes where competent professionals – trained specifically in Bahá'í educational practice and using first-class facilities and equipment – will shape them into the citizens of tomorrow's world. First we must strive to establish children's classes in our areas.

The Bahá'í teacher has a great part to play in Bahá'í life and is worthy of our respect and wholehearted support, no matter how undeveloped our education system may yet be. Because the teacher has a relationship with the child second only to that of the parents themselves, he or she is like a member of the family, for to the teacher do we entrust part of the spiritual development of our children.

Training Children to Consult

Consultation is a skill which can be introduced to children as soon as they become 'verbal'. In fact, the sooner the better, for, left to their own devices, bad habits are established which are later very difficult to change: criticism and ridicule, name calling, power plays and blackmailing are soon seized upon in order to coerce others into a desired behaviour. As we have seen in Chapter Six, the example of the parents is very important. If the children observe the parents regularly consulting and if they themselves are frequently included in family consultation, the children will see that Bahá'í consultation really does resolve problems peacefully and equitably. They will also acquire many of the principles of consultation through the power of example. If the skills involved are taught little by little in a consistent and rewarding way, the children will naturally develop the habit of consultation in their relationships with others.

Such skills are best practised in a non-threatening situation; it is not a good idea to introduce them at the height of an all-out skirmish. Rather, a start can be made by deciding what to do on the weekend or by discussing some other similar matter.

The first principle to establish could be the principle of listening to the others and really trying to understand. If the child can trust the other party to listen and care, this immediately becomes a rewarding situation for him. This satisfies in part the first condition of consultation which is that of unity, love and harmony. The parent of even a little child can take the time to listen to a sobbed account of toys snatched and not returned, of grazed knees and biting puppies. The most vital aspect of teaching the value of consultation is the spirit in which it takes place, a spirit which reassures the child that he is important to the others taking part and that his needs and thoughts will be heard and respected.

If a regular opportunity for family consultation is provided – for example, one evening a week after dinner – new skills can be introduced and practised one at a time. For adults to be reminded of these skills from time to time is an assistance in bringing those aspects to the forefront of their consciousness. Older children might be able to research the Writings and make a list of the principles involved. These can then be introduced one at a time during the regular family consultation and can be a family goal to be achieved over the following week until it is time for a new principle to be introduced.

Preparing Children to Serve Humanity

The station of man is that of a servant and it is through service that our true happiness lies. The child should be encouraged to consider the needs of others and to serve them in ways suited to his or her ability and capacity. At first these lessons will be practised within the family as the

child fulfils tasks and functions which are for the betterment of the family as a whole, while being encouraged to
see that he or she is an important and appreciated member
of the family. Little by little, the child can be enabled to
serve outside the family, perhaps having the privilege of
serving the local Bahá'í community in some way. One
child might be able to assist regularly the local secretary in
addressing envelopes for the monthly newsletter, another
might assist the librarian by covering library books. In the
local neighbourhood one child might offer to take out an
elderly neighbour's rubbish bin regularly or mow her
lawns. These activities should only take place as the child
is able to see them as important responsibilities to be
valued, never from a sense of compulsion, for it is the
spirit of these services which gives them life.

The Role of Youth

> This Cause, although it embraces with equal esteem people
> of all ages, has a special message and mission for the youth
> of your generation. It is their charter for their future, their
> hope, their guarantee of better days to come.[13]

At a time when so many youth feel overwhelmed by
hopelessness and fear, the Bahá'í youth provide a sharp
contrast – full of confidence, energy and enthusiasm,
frustrated only by lack of direction and opportunity if no
channel for this zeal is open to them. It is a time of life
relatively free of restricting responsibilities or cloistered
dependence, and consequently the Bahá'í youth are ideally
suited to many types of teaching. During holidays they
can travel teach, preparing advance itineraries and organizing
the basic planning with minimal parental assistance. They
can take part in team teaching, practising organization
skills, group consultation and cooperation, using special
strengths such as musical ability, public speaking skills,

affinity with minority groups, ability in giving deepenings or working with children to strengthen the work of the team as a whole.

A youth may be able to pioneer, even attending school or university while resident in a goal area. Participation in periodic youth conferences will help youth develop skills which will enable them to serve in more effective ways, to develop confidence in their abilities to identify with others in similar situations and to learn from others' experiences. The period of youth is in many ways a very crucial period through which parents should guide their young people with wisdom and sensitivity, bearing in mind that:

> For any person, whether Bahá'í or not, his youthful years are those in which he will make many decisions which will set the course of his life. In these years he is most likely to choose his life's work, complete his education, begin to earn his own living, marry, and start to raise his own family. Most important of all, it is during this period that the mind is most questing and that the spiritual values that will guide the person's future behaviour are adopted.[14]

Obligatory Prayer and Fasting

The age of fifteen is given as the beginning of maturity at which time the child should begin the observance of obligatory prayer and fasting. This should be a time of real significance for the young person and his family and one which many families may choose to mark in some suitably befitting manner. It should be preceded by thoughtful preparation, for these are acts of great spiritual significance and the manner in which they are embarked upon should reflect such an attitude. If there are several youth of a similar age in the community, perhaps preparatory activities could be arranged. Youth at this time of their lives appreciate being able to share their thoughts and experiences with

others in the same situation. Attendance at youth conferences and similar gatherings are important and valuable
experiences for these young people who feel part adult,
part child yet find it difficult at times to identify fully with
either group. Communities could mark this 'coming of
age' in a special way. Perhaps the Local Spiritual Assembly
could meet with the young person and make a small
presentation. The local newsletter might make a special
mention of the occasion and the community could hold a
special social event.

Preparation for the Spiritual Responsibilities of Maturity

The purpose of the education of the child is to make him
or her an independent adult. At the age of fifteen the youth
must become responsible for his or her own spiritual
development. He or she must fulfil all the obligations
which God expects of the adult: regular prayer and reading
of the Sacred verses, observance of daily obligatory
prayers and the Fast, observance of the laws, giving to the
Fund and other obligations which constitute firmness in
the Covenant. Although each child is an individual and
will advance only at his or her own pace, each needs to be
ready when the time comes to undertake these responsibilities of his or her volition and with as much preparation
and assistance as is required to be fitted for this milestone.

This is also a milestone for the parents: responsibility for
the spiritual development of the child has now been
discharged. Although a special relationship of concern and
support will always be there, the youth is stepping out
alone into the spiritual world, dependent only on God.

Gradually the bonds of material dependency are removed.
Soon the youth will share with the parents the privilege of
contributing financially to the costs of the home. He or she

will play a greater part in the responsibilities of day-to-day family living and will make more independent choices and decisions concerning his or her life. This is often a difficult time for the family. It is difficult for parents, who have spent the best part of two decades shouldering a weighty responsibility, to adjust to a new phase in their relationship with the person they will always think of as their child. The youth may be either impatient or reluctant to acquire new responsibilities. It is a period when balance, moderation and timeliness are so important. The reins of responsibility need to be passed over at the right time, in the right areas, in the right way. The parents are often reluctant to do this in case the youth is not yet ready. The youth is often frustrated and impatient to experience independence and to make his or her own choices.

The Bahá'í family which has developed close consultation and mutual trust and respect among its members will find this a time of great fulfilment. The blossoms borne on the tree of the family are bearing their fruit. It is a time of gratitude and celebration. The parents have been honoured by raising a child of the Kingdom who will carry forward the purpose of God for humankind. The youth will forever honour the parents who have sacrificed and laboured to bring him or her up in the knowledge and love of God. Humanity itself has been enriched. The purpose of marriage has been fulfilled.

> He is God! O peerless Lord! In Thine almighty wisdom Thou hast enjoined marriage upon the peoples, that the generations of men may succeed one another in this contingent world, and that ever, so long as the world shall last, they may busy themselves at the Threshold of Thy oneness with servitude and worship, with salutation, adoration and praise.[15]

References

1. Introductory Perspectives

1. Based on a concept outlined in John Kolstoe, *Consultation: A Universal Lamp of Guidance* (Oxford: George Ronald), 1985.
2. Matt. 7:24–7.
3. Shoghi Effendi in *Family Life*, p. 24.
4. Shoghi Effendi, *World Order*. p. 156.
5. Shoghi Effendi in *Centres of Bahá'í Learning*, p. 2.
6. Shoghi Effendi, *Dawn of a New Day*, p. 48.
7. Shoghi Effendi in *Heaven of Divine Wisdom*, p. 11.
8. Shoghi Effendi, *God Passes By*, p. 281.

2. The Place of the Family in the World Order

1. *By-Laws of a Local Spiritual Assembly*. See *Bahá'í World*, vol. XVII (1976–1979), p. 361.
2. The Universal House of Justice, *Constitution*, p. 4.
3. Shoghi Effendi in *Local Spiritual Assembly*, p. 16.
4. The Universal House of Justice, *Five Year Plan Message*.
5. 'Abdu'l-Bahá, *Promulgation*, p. 157.
6. ibid. p. 142.
7. Shoghi Effendi, *Citadel,* pp. 130–1.
8. 'Abdu'l-Bahá in *Bahá'í Prayers*, p. 107.
9. ibid. p. 106.
10. 'Abdu'l-Bahá, *Selections*, pp. 117–18.
11. ibid. p. 118.
12. Bahá'u'lláh in *Bahá'í Prayers*, p. 105.
13. The Universal House of Justice in *Family Life*, pp.29–30.
14. 'Abdu'l-Bahá, *Selections*, p. 279.
15. Shoghi Effendi in *Family Life*, p. 16.

16. Bahá'u'lláh, *Tablets*, p. 128.
17. 'Abdu'l-Bahá in *Bahá'í Education*, p. 35.
18. ibid.
19. Blomfield, *Chosen Highway*, pp. 39–40.
20. Honnold, *Vignettes*, pp. 81–2.

3. Unity and Diversity within the Family

1. Shoghi Effendi, *Dawn of a New Day*, p. 86.
2. 'Abdu'l-Bahá, *Paris Talks*, p. 183.
3. The Universal House of Justice in *Family Life*, p. 32.
4. 'Abdu'l-Bahá in *Bahá'í World Faith*, p. 411.
5. 'Abdu'l-Bahá in *Family Life*, p. 30.
6. ibid. pp. 30–3.
7. ibid. p. 31.
8. ibid.
9. 'Abdu'l-Bahá, *Paris Talks*, p. 183.
10. 'Abdu'l-Bahá in *Family Life*, p. 32.
11. ibid.
12. ibid. p. 31.
13. ibid.
14. 'Abdu'l-Bahá, *Selections*, p. 126.
15. 'Abdu'l-Bahá in *Family Life*, p. 31.
16. ibid. p. 32.
17. ibid. p. 31.
18. Bahá'u'lláh in ibid. p. 1.
19. 'Abdu'l-Bahá, *Some Answered Questions*, p. 231.
20. 'Abdu'l-Bahá, *Tablets*, vol. 2, p. 463.
21. 'Abdu'l-Bahá, *Some Answered Questions*, pp. 231–2.
22. Shoghi Effendi in *Family Life*, p. 23.
23. 'Abdu'l-Bahá in ibid. p. 31.
24. 'Abdu'l-Bahá, *Promulgation*, p. 168.

4. Implementing the Equality of Men and Women

1. 'Abdu'l-Bahá in *Women*, pp. 11–12.
2. 'Abdu'l-Bahá, *Promulgation*, p. 375.
3. 'Abdu'l-Bahá, *Paris Talks*, p. 161.
4. ibid. p. 162.
5. ibid. p. 163.

6. 'Abdu'l-Bahá in *Women*, p. 41.
7. 'Abdu'l-Bahá, *Promulgation*, p. 76.
8. 'Abdu'l-Bahá, *Paris Talks*, p. 163.
9. 'Abdu'l-Bahá in *Women*, pp. 11–12.
10. 'Abdu'l-Bahá, *Promulgation*, p. 284.
11. 'Abdu'l-Bahá in *Women*, p. 4.
12. 'Abdu'l-Bahá, *Paris Talks*, p. 162.
13. 'Abdu'l-Bahá in *Women*, p. 12.
14. 'Abdu'l-Bahá, *Promulgation*, p. 375.
15. 'Abdu'l-Bahá, *Paris Talks*, p. 183.
16. ibid. p. 184.
17. 'Abdu'l-Bahá, *Promulgation*, p. 284.
18. 'Abdu'l-Bahá in *Women*, p. 42.
19. ibid. pp. 35–6.
20. The Universal House of Justice in *Women*, p. 30.
21. ibid.
22. 'Abdu'l-Bahá, *Promulgation*, pp. 76–7.
23. 'Abdu'l-Bahá in *Women*, p. 42.
24. The Universal House of Justice in ibid. p. 50.

5. Families in Transition

1. 'Abdu'l-Bahá, *Foundations*, p. 61.
2. Shoghi Effendi in *Lights*, no. 1870, p. 550.
3. 'Abdu'l-Bahá, *Selections*, p. 118.
4. 'Abdu'l-Bahá cited in *Star*, vol. 13, pp. 227–8.
5. Shoghi Effendi, *World Order*, p. 204.
6. Shoghi Effendi in *Lights*, no. 2106, p. 623.
7. ibid. no 2115, p. 625.
8. Shoghi Effendi, *Living the Life*, p. 18.

6. Family Consultation as a Tool for Progress

1. 'Abdu'l-Bahá, *Some Answered Questions*, p. 233.
2. 'Bahá'u'lláh in *Heaven of Divine Wisdom*, p. 3.
3. The Universal House of Justice in *Family Life*, p. 30.
4. Gibran, *Prophet*.
5. Bahá'u'lláh in *Bahá'í Education*, p. 2.
6. 'Abdu'l-Bahá, *Promulgation*, p. 142.
7. 'Abdu'l-Bahá, *Foundations*, p. 26.
8. 'Abdu'l-Bahá, *Divine Civilization*, p. 19.

9. 'Abdu'l-Bahá, *Foundations*, p. 101.
10. 'Abdu'l-Bahá in *Bahá'í Education*, p. 53.
11. Bahá'u'lláh, *Tablets*, p. 27.
12. ibid. p. 66.
13. 'Abdu'l-Bahá in *Bahá'í Education*, p. 54.

7. The Education of Children

1. See *Lights*, nos. 1160–3, pp. 345–7.
2. 'Abdu'l-Bahá, *Tablets*, vol. 3, p. 579.
3. 'Abdu'l-Bahá, *Selections*, pp. 126–7.
4. 'Abdu'l-Bahá, *Paris Talks*, pp. 109–10.
5. 'Abdu'l-Bahá, *Selections*, p. 135.
6. 'Abdu'l-Bahá cited in Maxwell, *Early Pilgrimage*, p. 42.
7. Shoghi Effendi *Living the Life*, p. 29.
8. 'Abdu'l-Bahá, *Promulgation*, p. 134.
9. 'Abdu'l-Bahá in *Bahá'í Education*, p. 52.
10. ibid. p. 51.
11. Shoghi Effendi in ibid. p. 72.
12. 'Abdu'l-Bahá, *Promulgation*, p. 283.
13. 'Abdu'l-Bahá, *Some Answered Questions*, p. 8.
14. 'Abdu'l-Bahá in *Bahá'í Education*, p. 52.
15. 'Abdu'l-Bahá, *Selections*, p. 129.
16. ibid.
17. ibid.
18. Bahá'u'lláh, *Tablets*, p. 128.
19. 'Abdu'l-Bahá, *Selections*, p. 127.
20. ibid. p. 129.
21. ibid.
22. 'Abdu'l-Bahá in *Bahá'í Education*, p. 83.
23. 'Abdu'l-Bahá, *Promulgation*, p. 52.
24. 'Abdu'l-Bahá, *Selections*, p. 159.
25. ibid. p. 124.
26. 'Abdu'l-Bahá, *Some Answered Questions*, p. 8.
27. 'Abdu'l-Bahá, *Selections*, p. 127.
28. 'Abdu'l-Bahá, *Tablets*, vol. 3, p. 579.

8. Divine Education

1. Bahá'u'lláh in *Bahá'í Education*, p. 4.
2. 'Abdu'l-Bahá in *Family Life*, p. 9–10.

3. 'Abdu'l-Bahá in *Bahá'í Education*, pp. 42–3.
4. Shoghi Effendi in ibid. p. 78.
5. Bahá'u'lláh in *Family Life*, p. 1.
6. Shoghi Effendi in *Importance of Prayer*, p. 15.
7. 'Abdu'l-Bahá in *Bahá'í Education*, p. 42.
8. ibid.
9. Shoghi Effendi in *Bahá'í Administration*, p. 66.
10. Shoghi Effendi in *Bahá'í Education*, p. 77.
11. 'Abdu'l-Bahá in ibid. p. 11.
12. The Universal House of Justice, letter of 25 May 1975 to the Bahá'ís of the World.
13. Shoghi Effendi in *Lights*, no. 2125, p. 628.
14. The Universal House of Justice, *Wellspring*, p. 92–3.
15. Bahá'u'lláh in *Bahá'í Prayers*, pp. 105–6.

Bibliography

'Abdu'l-Bahá. *Foundations of World Unity.* Wilmette, Illinois: Bahá'í Publishing Trust, 1974.
—— *Paris Talks.* Oakham: Bahá'í Publishing Trust, 1969.
—— *The Promulgation of Universal Peace.* Compiled by Howard MacNutt. Wilmette, Illinois: Bahá'í Publishing Trust, 2nd ed. 1982.
—— *The Secret of Divine Civilization.* Translated by Marzieh Gail. Wilmette, Illinois: Bahá'í Publishing Trust, 1957.
—— *Selections from the Writings of 'Abdu'l-Bahá.* Translated by a Committee at the Bahá'í World Centre and by Marzieh Gail. Haifa: Bahá'í World Centre, 1987.
—— *Some Answered Questions.* Collected and translated from the Persian by Laura Clifford Barney. Wilmette, Illinois: Bahá'í Publishing Trust, 1981.
—— *Tablets of 'Abdu'l-Bahá,* 3 vols. New York: Bahá'í Publishing Committee, 1930–40.
Bahá'í Education. Compilation issued by the Universal House of Justice. Oakham: Bahá'í Publishing Trust, 1976.
Bahá'í Prayers: A Selection of Prayers. Wilmette, Illinois: Bahá'í Publishing Trust, 1982.
Bahá'í World, The. Reprinted. Wilmette, Illinois: Bahá'í Publishing Trust, 1980.
Bahá'í World Faith. Wilmette, Illinois: Bahá'í Publishing Trust, rev. ed. 1976.
Bahá'u'lláh. *Tablets of Bahá'u'lláh revealed after the Kitáb-i-Aqdas.* Compiled by the Research Department of the Universal House of Justice and translated by Habib Taherzadeh with the assistance of a Committee at the Bahá'í World Centre. Haifa: Bahá'í World Centre, 1978.
Blomfield, Lady. *The Chosen Highway.* Wilmette, Illinois: Bahá'í Publishing Trust, 1967.

Centers of Bahá'í Learning. Compilation issued by the Universal House of Justice. Wilmette, Illinois: Bahá'í Publishing Trust, 1980.

Family Life. Compilation issued by the Universal House of Justice. Oakham: Bahá'í Publishing Trust, 1982.

Gibran, Kahlil. *The Prophet.* London: Heinemann, 1980.

The Heaven of Divine Wisdom. Compilation issued by the Universal House of Justice. Oakham: Bahá'í Publishing Trust, 1978.

Honnold, Annamarie. *Vignettes from the Life of 'Abdu'l-Bahá.* Oxford: George Ronald, 1982.

Hornby, Helen. *Lights of Guidance: A Bahá'í Reference File.* New Delhi, India: Bahá'í Publishing Trust, 1983.

The Importance of Prayer, Meditation and the Devotional Attitude. Oakham: Bahá'í Publishing Trust, 1982.

The Local Spiritual Assembly. Oakham: Bahá'í Publishing Trust, 1970.

Maxwell, May. *An Early Pilgrimage.* Rev. edn. Oxford: George Ronald, 1969.

Shoghi Effendi. *Bahá'í Administration: Selected Messages 1922–1932.* Wilmette, Illinois: Bahá'í Publishing Trust, 1974.

—— *Citadel of Faith: Messages to America 1947–1957.* Wilmette, Illinois: Bahá'í Publishing Trust, 1965.

—— *Dawn of a New Day: Messages to India 1923–1957.* Delhi: Bahá'í Publishing Trust, 1970.

—— *God Passes By.* Wilmette, Illinois: Bahá'í Publishing Trust, 1944.

—— *Living the Life.* Oakham: Bahá'í Publishing Trust, 1974.

—— *The World Order of Bahá'u'lláh.* Wilmette, Illinois: Bahá'í Publishing Trust, 1969.

Star of the West. Reprinted in 8 volumes. Oxford: George Ronald, 1984.

The Universal House of Justice. *The Constitution of the Universal House of Justice.* Haifa: Bahá'í World Centre, 1972.

—— Letter to all National Spiritual Assemblies, 25 May 1975.

—— Letter to the Bahá'ís of the World announcing the Five Year Plan, Naw-Rúz 1979.

—— *Wellspring of Guidance: Messages 1963–1968.* Wilmette, Illinois: Bahá'í Publishing Trust, 1969.

Women. Compilation issued by the Universal House of Justice. Oakham: Bahá'í Publishing Trust, 1986.

www.ingramcontent.com/pod-product-compliance
Lightning Source LLC
Chambersburg PA
CBHW031300090426
42742CB00007B/540